THE STORY OF THE CAMPERVAN

ANDREW JENKINSON

AMBERLEY

This book is dedicated to my lifelong photographer friends,
Peter and Edwin – two great buddies!

Image Credits

Chapter 3
Courtesy of John Lunt: pp. 54, 55, 56 (top), 57 (middle and bottom) and 58

Chapter 4
Courtesy of Andrew Jenkinson Photography: pp. 88 (top), 91 (bottom), 92, 93, 94 and 95 (bottom)

Courtesy of David Elliot Wellhouse Leisure: p. 89

First published 2025

Amberley Publishing
The Hill, Stroud,
Gloucestershire, GL5 4EP

www.amberley-books.com

ISBN: 978 1 3981 1871 3 (print)
ISBN: 978 1 3981 1872 0 (ebook)

British Library Cataloguing in Publication Data.
A catalogue record for this book is available from the British Library.

Typeset in 10pt on 13pt Celeste.
Typesetting by SJmagic DESIGN SERVICES, India.
Printed in the UK.

CONTENTS

PREFACE

The campervan has become one of the most popular leisure vehicles on the road. With modern base vehicles with car-like manners, the campervan market has particularly grown over the last decade. This is the story of how the campervan has evolved from the 1950s to the modern day. It explores how folk used them, where they went and how the early campervan user was seen as being slightly eccentric, sleeping and eating in what was essentially a van with a bed and cooker in it!

The person in the street will often describe a campervan as a 'Dormobile or Caravanette', both old brand names from years gone by. A bit like Hoover when they mean a vacuum cleaner! The VW has always been a popular campervan conversion, with converters from the early days noting the VW as a good base vehicle to use. In the 1960s and 1970s these rather noisy and sluggish vans were used by many converters. Here I examine the best-known and lesser-known makes and designs and their development over the decades. Although this is not a full A to Z of campervan makes and models, this book details how the campervan has progressed through images from my archive and a few other sources. So, pop the kettle on, make yourself comfy and discover this leisure vehicle's heritage – a truly nostalgic trip that will simply amaze you!

Andrew Jenkinson, caravan, motorhome and campervan journalist
and historian and YouTube channel caravan industry expert

1

SLEEPING IN A DELIVERY VAN?

The campervan was to be the new leisure vehicle of the 1950s. Following the Second World War, the motor industry had begun to explore new avenues in vehicle design and practicalities. The shooting brake (estate car or, in the US, station wagon) had grown in popularity by the 1930s. This stretched version of a standard car by a maker involved providing extra space for those who had a large family or a taxi business, for example. Some owners also used them as an emergency place to sleep while away and dropping the rear seats provided a large area to lie down on. Sleeping in a car was usually done by folk waiting for a ferry or needing to drive off early the next day.

This image from the 1930s shows an extension to a car – was this the birth of the conversion?

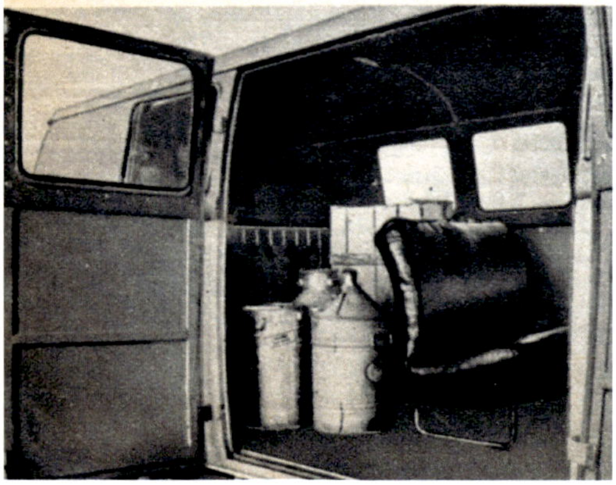

The 1950 VW Kombi started the conversion ball rolling when in 1952 Westfalia saw its potential as sleeping accommodation with their Camping Box design.

In defeated Germany the task of rebuilding was not going to be an easy one. Factories lay in ruins with businesses having long ceased trading. There was an influx of US and British people who began the task of rebuilding the economy in West Germany. The VW factory was cleared and reorganised to design and build cars. The Beetle was to come back into production and a new vehicle was to be added, a cross between a car and a small bus. Named the VW Microbus, or the Type 2, this rear-engine vehicle could carry several passengers and also convert to a delivery-type vehicle. It was designed by Dutchman Ben Pon.

Westfalia, the German trailer-caravan producer, saw the potential of this vehicle in the early 1950s when the VW was launched. They looked into making it usable for sleeping and cooking in but also to be converted back to a conventional passenger vehicle for daily use. In 1952 Westfalia designed and made a conversion kit, naming it the Camping Box. The kit allowed the interior of the VW to be made into living accommodation but could then be taken out so the vehicle was returned to normal use. The Westfalia Camping Box conversion became a success and the company further developed and converted the VW. By the mid-1960s Westfalia had dropped caravan production to concentrate on VW campervan conversions.

The VW was seen as an ideal vehicle to convert, proving to be tough, reliable and easy to adapt. As a result, in the 1960s it became the top choice of converters in the UK, although development was a little slower there. Dormobile, the name that came to be used by the public to describe a campervan, was one of the first campervan manufacturers in the UK. Martin-Walter Ltd, based in Folkestone, Kent, was founded in 1774, producing harnesses, horse-drawn coaches and later vehicle bodies in the 1900s. After the Second World War Walter's converted a few Austin Tens to sleep a person, but that was it. However, in the early 1950s one of Walter's directors, Spencer Apps, took the idea further. With the introduction of the new generation of compact, pressed-steel-shell delivery vans he noticed a potential further use.

Pre-Dormobile trademark parent company Martin-Walter at first converted small estate cars that could be slept in.

The Bedford CA was utilised by Dormobile and followed by other new converters.

Walter's had been keen to adapt the Bedford CA to carry passengers – a minibus in effect. Apps had seen cars and vans parking up overnight to catch a ferry and observed that owners were sleeping in them. After studying the design of the new CA, he realised that a coach-building company such as Walter's could make a short-wheelbase CA with the ability to adapt the daytime seats into beds. The idea was born and in 1952 Walter's brought its sleeper van to market. It was decided that a brand name was needed. Another director of the firm, Lyne Smith, thought hard about this versatile vehicle and came up with the Latin-derived name of Dormobile. This was adopted and went on to become universally known.

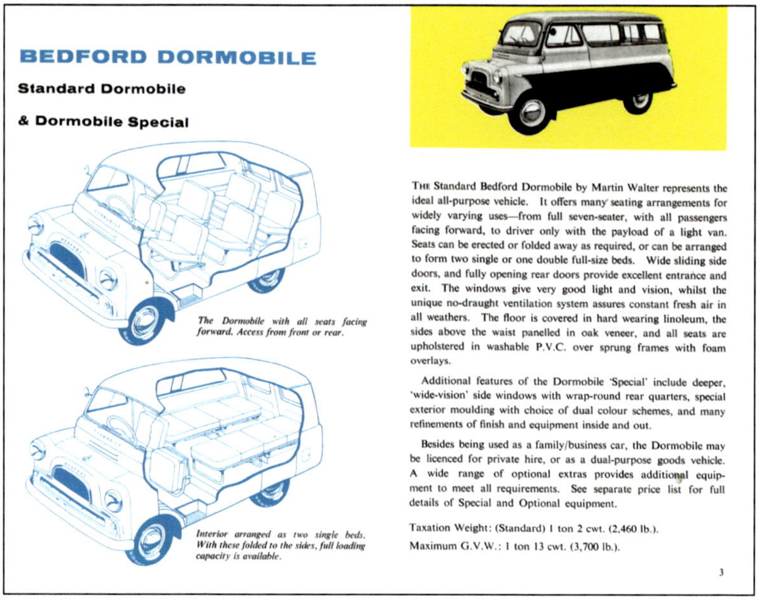

BEDFORD DORMOBILE

Standard Dormobile

& Dormobile Special

The Dormobile with all seats facing forward. Access from front or rear.

Interior arranged as two single beds. With these folded to the sides, full loading capacity is available.

THE Standard Bedford Dormobile by Martin Walter represents the ideal all-purpose vehicle. It offers many seating arrangements for widely varying uses—from full seven-seater, with all passengers facing forward, to driver only with the payload of a light van. Seats can be erected or folded away as required, or can be arranged to form two single or one double full-size beds. Wide sliding side doors, and fully opening rear doors provide excellent entrance and exit. The windows give very good light and vision, whilst the unique no-draught ventilation system assures constant fresh air in all weathers. The floor is covered in hard wearing linoleum, the sides above the waist panelled in oak veneer, and all seats are upholstered in washable P.V.C. over sprung frames with foam overlays.

Additional features of the Dormobile 'Special' include deeper, 'wide-vision' side windows with wrap-round rear quarters, special exterior moulding with choice of dual colour schemes, and many refinements of finish and equipment inside and out.

Besides being used as a family/business car, the Dormobile may be licenced for private hire, or as a dual-purpose goods vehicle. A wide range of optional extras provides additional equipment to meet all requirements. See separate price list for full details of Special and Optional equipment.

Taxation Weight: (Standard) 1 ton 2 cwt. (2,460 lb.).

Maximum G.V.W.: 1 ton 13 cwt. (3,700 lb.).

3

Two Dormobile designs with the Bedford CA from the mid-1950s.

The Dormobile Bedford CA with the trademark pram open-roof extension and candy-stripe finish.

The early designs proved to be uncomfortable to sleep in, involving folding both the front and rear seats down to form a bed. The beds were also narrow but a company such as Walter's were able to improve the sleeping arrangements. To offer extended headroom in the Dormobile, as it will be referred to from now on, the company designed a new elevating roof which folded up on one hinge and had the Dormobile candy-stripe finish. Based on Bedford's CA delivery van, this conversion with a 1.6 petrol-engine, just three gears and a smaller bonnet felt car-like to drive. Now folk didn't need to have a car and pull a trailer caravan, they could utilise one vehicle. The new Dormobile Bedford campervan featured an onboard water tank, underfloor gas-bottle storage, kitchen and wardrobe.

Put into production, the Dormobile was soon stocked by garages and further development moved quite quickly. Dormobile had also converted the beloved Morris Minor 5 cwt van and the early Morris J Type, but these were basically a bed on wheels and not very flexible. With the launch of the Bedford CA, other new lightweight vans came onto the market: Austin/Morris 152/J2, Ford Thames, Standard Atlas and, of course, the infamous VW. Dormobile, though, stuck with the Bedford CA and designed kitchen and storage facilities into the compact dimensions. Using a GRP moulded top roof section, Dormobile with the roof up meant that users could now stand up and not have to stoop as well as having an additional bed!

Two-tone paintwork makes this an attractive campervan for its time. Dormobile developed their conversions quickly as demand grew.

A typical Dormobile interior. Small families found the Bedford compact but practical in use.

Other models came onto the scene including Caravette, a VW-based conversion built by Devon-based J. P. White Ltd. The name Caravette, like Dormobile, was used to describe any conversion of a van! In the late 1950s Moortown Motors, based in Leeds, began using the VW Kombi. Moortown produced several models offering a variety of layouts. The Moortown campervans were well designed and practical and were advertised as being ideal for families and for the travelling rep, who could also hold meetings in

Above: A new conversion on a VW was done by Moortown in Leeds, though the conversion was carried out by specialist caravan maker Balmforth from Malton.

Right: Moortown had several layout designs. The one pictured here required fine weather with a two-burner cooker on one door and a tiny sink on the opposite one.

Left: Maurice Calthorpe supplied several early converters with this excellent elevating roof section.

Below: Peter Pitt claimed he was the first true UK converter using the VW. He went on to use the Austin J4 and the Ford Thames, as pictured here.

the roomy central lounge. To create extra headroom, Moortown adopted the best roof design available, manufactured by Calthorpe, which also supplied other converters. The Moortown was not converted by the company but by a caravan manufacturer. Balmforth Caravans, based in Malton, North Yorkshire, was well known for quality caravans, as well as fairground showmen's ornate vans. The company didn't produce motorhomes or campervans but converted for Moortown; Balmforth shut in 1967 after over sixty years in business.

In the late 1950s new lightweight commercial vans began appearing on the market and these offered ideal opportunities for the new campervan market, which was still very much in its infancy. Moto-Caravan was another maker and, again, its name was used to describe a van conversion. At this company, Peter Pitt considered the VW Transporter (but used Ford and BMC soon after) because he thought its handling was more car-like but, if that was the case, he questioned why the converted van was still restricted to 30 mph and subject to purchase tax. The touring caravan, however, was not subject to purchase tax. Pitt would use the Austin J4 as a base, too, and the Ford Thames, both of which offered different qualities in Pitt's eyes.

Using one of his campervans, Pitt drove through the Royal Park at Windsor, where commercial vehicles were exempt from tax. He was stopped by police and in court Pitt set out his case and the campervan was thereafter treated as a car. Pitt produced innovative designs and in 1958/9 added a roof-top tent as an extra bedroom for an additional £59. Pitt's ideas included a front single bed utilising the two front van seats, although other

Pitt's designs were very practical and he used space extremely well. Okay, who is sleeping on the roof tonight? The roof tent was an optional extra, though few were sold.

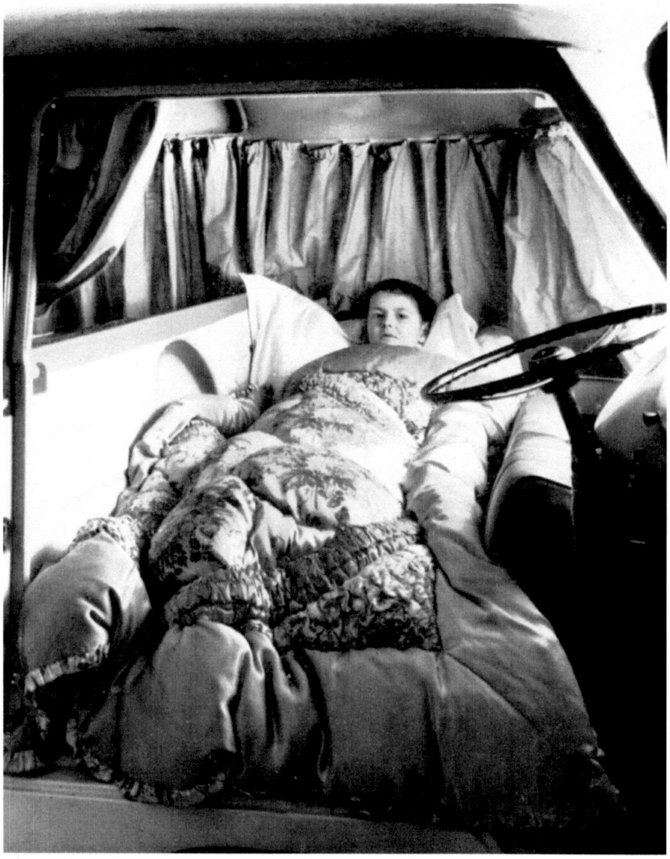

Above left: Are you comfortable, son? The front wasn't ideal, but it served a purpose as a single bed for a child.

Above right: Another idea was a double bed at the front, as seen in this 1959 conversion.

Left: Pitt's talent for designing a conversion to maximise space is demonstrated by this dinette in a Morris van.

converters also offered this and it was in fact more suitable for children than adults due to size restrictions. He was clever with his use of space, making his conversions feel roomy through placing items such as the cooker and sink on the rear or side doors. In the 1960s Pitt joined Canterbury Products and here he was given free rein to develop his ideas, although sadly he received very little income from this venture.

The next campervan brand that would make waves was the Home Cruiser. Designed by Maurice Calthorpe, the roof extension was simple in that it pushed up to form a curved roof with wooden sides, although the roof itself was formed of metal sheet. The roof was easy to operate and offered excellent headroom. As the market expanded, other converters became interested in Calthorpe's design and he sold it to other converters to use. Calthorpe

Above left: The dinette could be made into a decent-sized double bed with minimal fuss.

Above right: The late 1950s would see new converter Maurice Calthorpe launch the elevating roof Home Cruiser, using the Morris.

The interior of Calthorpe's Home Cruiser. The conversion was carried out by long-gone caravan maker Normandie with the interior specification to a high standard. Note a full oven and supplementary gas light.

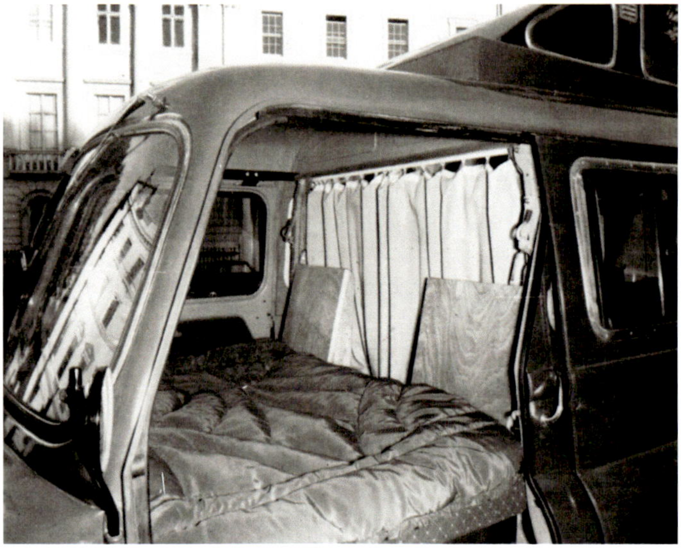

Left: The Home Cruiser with its version of a front-cab double-bed conversion from 1958.

Below: By the end of the 1950s Dormobile dominated the market, though small new converters were beginning to offer more competition.

also used the front cab in the Morris to make a double bed. Dormobile stuck with their fold-over roof extension, termed an elevating roof. The bold candy-colour lines used became an established trademark of Dormobile campervans, which became popular with buyers for their practical design and layouts and use of the Bedford CA.

Another Kent maker also using Bedford CAs was Kenex of Dover. Regarded as soundly designed campervans, these vehicles had louvred windows at the rear and a vertical rising roof featuring red stripes. Kenex was to become a target for Dormobile, which eventually took over the firm and then dropped the Kenex name. The late

Kenex produced similar designs to Dormobile using Bedford's CA van. Dormobile would eventually buy out Kenex.

1950s saw the advent of the new panel vans, such as the Ford Thames van, and some of the few converters adopted the Thames, although with no side entry (an option) it did in some cases restrict its conversion. Both the look-alike Morris J2 and the Austin 152 (basically the same van) were being chosen by the new generation of campervan makers coming into the market in the 1960s. This period saw a boom in campervan sales with garages selling them as a sideline to their main car-sales business. Caravan dealerships were not keen on stocking motorhomes or campervans, hence they were left to car dealers at a time when there were many independent family-run car dealerships in existence.

The campervan of the 1950s was still basic with very little in the way of living luxuries. Compromised beds that often saw the occupant still having to sleep in the front cabin with a steering wheel across the bed were the norm. Dining and cooking areas were also cramped with often just a small gas cooker and a bowl for the sink provided, with bed making also not easy. The campervan, though, was to be improved and Dormobile have to take the credit for their development with other converters looking to them and then creating their own versions. Campervans of the time used 12-V courtesy lights so night use was a dim affair. Having said that, some manufacturers fitted gas lighting, which also featured in caravans of the period. It was mostly couples who used campervans, although families also favoured them, more often than not as extra accommodation alongside a separate tent in which mum and dad would sleep.

Of course, the DIY person might buy an old van to convert themselves, often saving them money. However, they had to have the basic skills, although at the time there were no laws in place regarding safety as there are today, and some home-converted vans would leave a lot to be desired. The idea of a caravan-styled vehicle that you could use as a daily commuter as well as a place to sleep on the road was nevertheless catching on. Sites often looked down at the campervan owner, wondering just how they enjoyed a weekend or longer holiday break in what was designed to be a delivery van!

The Caravan Club, as it was known back then, shunned the coach-built-bodied motorhome as well as the converted delivery van concept. Some sites would not accept home-built designs on site, so owners would drive to some quiet spot to stop for the night. Back in the 1950s you could still do this with a touring caravan and campervan owners took up this practice as well. This became popular with many campervan users, who completely ignored caravan parks and embraced what would today be termed 'wild camping'. The growth of the new-type delivery vans was a bonus to converters. With the law changed on tax and speed limit, the campervan was seen in more numbers, many buyers using them as day-to-day transport and yet, in a moment, having the ability to load up and be off somewhere. Campervans in most cases would fit on the driveway.

Several campervans stop on a stretch of land, 1959. This was something you could do with relative ease in the late 1950s.

There were a number of makers around but by the end of the 1950s Dormobile had become prolific. With its Bedford-based favourite the CA, the Dormobile was being used as a template by other converters. Dormobile went on to use VW and the Ford Thames as well as Bedford's CA. Pitt's Moto-Caravan converted the VW Kombi and was a success, but by the following decade he had added Ford and Commer. The overall sales figures for campervans at the time are not easy to access. Generally, however, sales were on the up as garages stocked brands such as Airborne J. P. White with the Devon using the VW Transporter as a base vehicle, which was gaining ground in conversions.

The campervan was usually a very clever design using every bit of space and some years later new models of these vans had larger designs that gave converters more choice with reagards to layout. The Dormobiles were Bedford CA users but would, like many converters, also employ the VW. There were a variety of elevating roofs available, some being difficult to operate and awkward in design. The other alternative was to put a new roof on the van, cutting off the original roof section and replacing it with a GRP moulded section, usually with windows in it. Glass fibre allowed the campervan's height to be fixed permanent; the user could stand up in this space and could dispense with messing around with an elevating roof.

The 1950s had become the decade of the establishment of the campervan and at the Motor Show at Earls Court cars and caravans were displayed alongside the odd campervan.

A new dedicated caravan show was staged in Earls Court in 1959. Several campervans were shown at the event and more shows emerged as the industry developed.

By 1959 a new show had been launched at Earls Court especially for the caravan and new motorhome and campervan. It focused on leisure-vehicle manufacture and helped showcase the campervan and expose the public to its virtues. Maurice Calthorpe showed his Home Cruiser campervan to the public at the Ideal Home Exhibition in London in 1957.

Calthorpe's patented extending roof top provided 2.5 metres of headroom in his Home Cruiser model. Although Calthorpe designed and marketed the Home Cruiser, he didn't produce it. That was left to a caravan manufacturer, Normandie Caravans, which built some tourers but mainly mobile homes. They also produced specials but, interestingly, the first Home Cruisers were built on a Bedford CA and were coach-built, although a few were built and van conversions were produced. The quality of the Home Cruisers was good, giving the feel of a caravan, thanks to Normandie's influence, of course.

Dormobile, which had converted the Bedford CA in the mid-1950s as a minibus that required seats to be folded down for beds, had by the end of that decade become a well-known maker of campervans. The public was aware of the brand, which inspired many to check out the campervan lifestyle. The new generation of these pressed-steel lightweight vans, although easy to drive, still could not compete with the comfort and handling of a car. Yet, most buyers overlooked these shortcomings and became wrapped up in the idea of the freedom of the road with no hotels or B&Bs to worry about.

The early vans were often quite noisy and braking was not as responsive as cars, while handling also left much to be desired with cornering being a particular unpleasant experience at speed. No insulation was added and ventilation wasn't the best either. But these drawbacks didn't stop new buyers of the campervan which was seen as a good cheap holiday and unlike caravans of that period, not stuck to a 30-mph speed limit. With

Many campervan owners would stop in pull-ins down back roads for an overnight stay, partly as the then Caravan Club didn't want them in the club.

just a handful of converters at the end of the 1950s, this would grow to over twenty-five during the 1960s. Peter Pitt, one of the early converters who began in 1956 on VW, was in 1961 acquired by Canterbury Side Cars Ltd, which would develop the brand and become Canterbury Campervans, gaining popularity over the coming years.

Storage in the early models could be limited, so users had to travel light, taking only essential items. With limited spec, the campervan was seen as a makeshift 'caravan' and yet sales were buoyant. The Caravan Club and the then-named Camping Club were still not keen to have motorhomes or campervans in their groups, although the Camping Club let them join but various rules and regulations did not make them feel welcome. The motorhome owner and campervan folk would need a voice to represent them. With hostilities from the Caravan Club in 1959 there was work being carried out to form a club dedicated to these leisure vehicles. The Motor Caravanners Club would be formed, and the over the following decade would provide the campervan and motorhome owner with much-needed support.

With converters selling the product as well as the idea to those who didn't quite know what campervans were about, the blurb used boasted of the versatility of this vehicle. Some makers tapped into this and promoted a variety of uses for the vehicle: as a mobile office, family transport, ideal for reps and ideal for picnics, especially if it rained! The seeds had been sown and with the help of larger dealers such as Turner's and Wilson's, which grew with the industry, the promotion of the great outdoors and 'go where you want' theme gained in popularity.

At the first Caravan Show at Earls Court in 1959 there were several converters who received excellent coverage, and this no doubt helped the movement. Martin-Walter's were building eighty Dormobile campervans a week, and this fell short of demand. So, by late 1959, to increase numbers a factory extension had been built, one of several extensions added over the following years. However, the next decade would see rapid expansion and also the real start of the home conversion.

2

THE 1960S – CAMPERVAN EXPLOSION

The Swinging Sixties would see a massive upturn in campervan sales, helped by the new larger vans that were becoming more popular with small companies in particular. The one-man business that often used an estate car now looked at a van for their business, enabling them to carry extra tools and materials. This then would have a knock-on effect on leisure vehicles, as this chapter will explore. The number of converters that began in this era would increase choice for the new campervan buyer. Again, some caravan manufacturers converted vans as more of a sideline, such as Creighton, a Lancashire-based caravan maker.

Stanley Creighton Binns was a true entrepreneur, designing boats, park homes, touring caravans, amphibious caravans, trailer tents, coach-built motorhomes, campervans and

The 1960s witnessed the emergence of more converters and a bigger take-up of customers, including more families. This van is a Kenex.

even an automatic swimming-pool cover and a dog poop scoop! I once met Stanley, who at the age of eighty was still looking at new ideas. In 1964 Creighton used a Ford Thames to convert into a campervan, producing these mainly to order. However, by the 1970s he had turned to the new Bedford CF for an alternative Creighton conversion. Some of the early original makers, such as Kenex and Peter Pitts' concern (Moto-Caravan), were taken over by larger, stronger converters.

Right: The Ford Thames was a van used by many including small new converter Creighton Binns, which mainly produced caravans and a successful range of boats.

Below: An early 1962 Canterbury Pitt Thames-based conversion. Peter Pitt had agreed a merger with Canterbury Products, a deal that sadly made him little money.

The formation of the Motor Caravanners Club in 1960 provided coach-built as well as campervan owners with a voice and a way of celebrating the joys of owning both types of vehicle. The club grew quickly. The then Caravan Club had been pressured to allow motorhomes and campervans to join their swelling ranks, though members had tried to veto the decision; at this time members had a say in most of what the club did.

Ironically, many years later, the Caravan Club would spend thousands of pounds on remarketing and changing its name to the Caravan and Motorhome Club! Although the price of a new conversion was around £800-plus in this era, a growing number of campervan users looked at buying a second-hand delivery van and then incorporating their own ideas and furniture, etc. For the most part, many of these home-built conversions were basic and often the vans were past their best, with body rust and worn engines requiring work.

The DIY segment, though, was seen by some as a positive addition to the campervan market. The idea was developed by a few small companies that made designs up for campervan DIY enthusiasts. They would supply plans for several van bases, such as the ever-popular VW, for around 16*s* (80p). A detailed set of instructions were sent out with accurate measurements and advice on materials to use. So, an owner could cut costs on

Fancy some self-build? In 1968 you could buy campervan conversion plans offering different layout options.

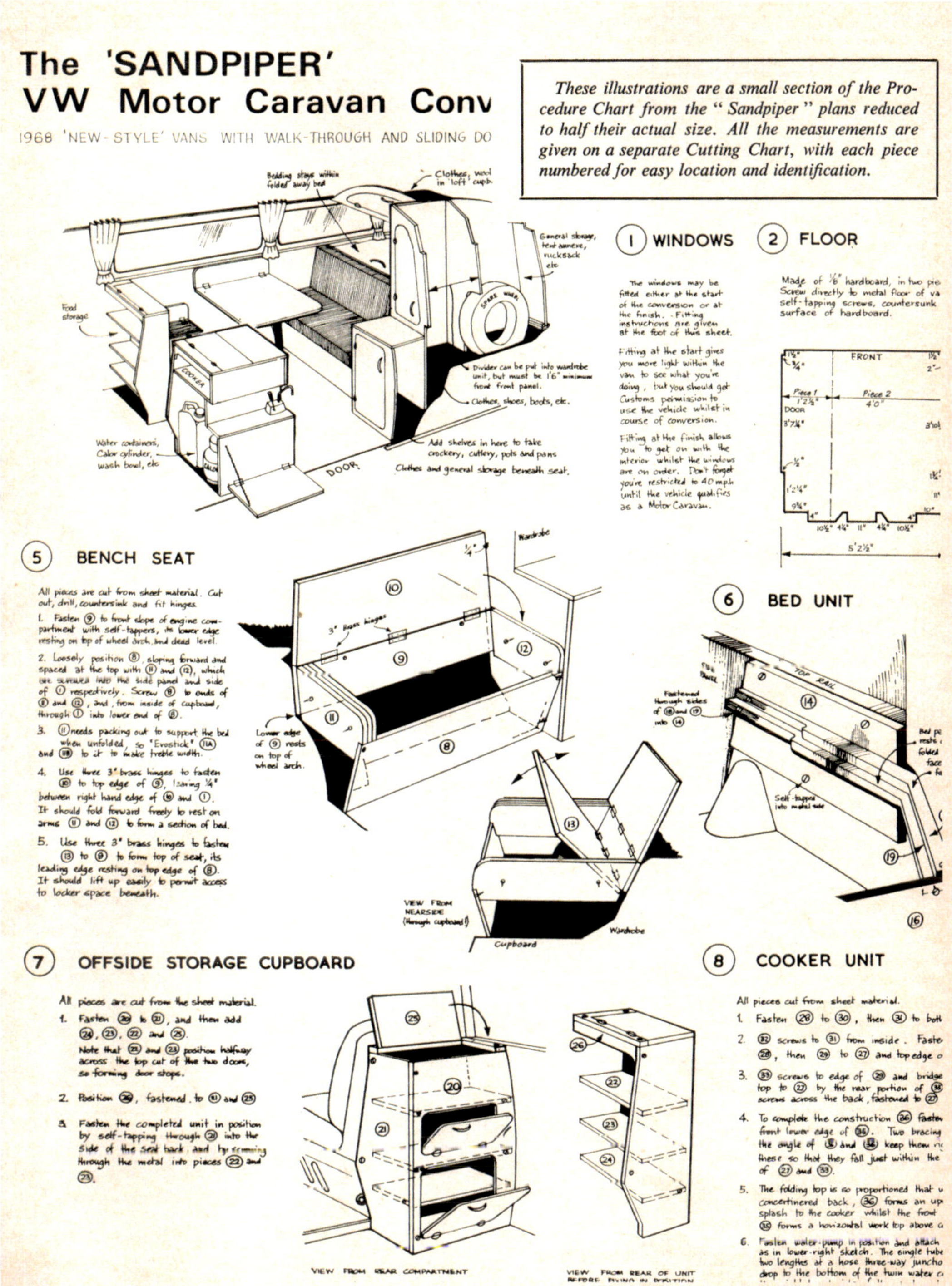

Plans for the VW T2, named the Sandpiper design. Costing 16s (80p), this could be a project to carry out over winter to then be ready for the off in spring.

owning a campervan, and, in fact, some dealers and manufacturers were founded on a self-build project that turned into a business. The most famous of these were Auto-Sleepers, Holdsworth, Leisure Drive and dealer Todd's Motorhomes, near Preston. These names had begun with a home conversion and resulted with a sale of the finished project. Cotswold maker Auto-Sleepers saw the Trevelyan family establish this company quite by accident. Based in the village of Willersey, in 1961 the family converted a Morris J4 to accommodate them touring around France. Using a basic side-raising roof for headroom, the interior finish was of a high standard (a trait of the brand) and soon enquiries saw the family start production with Auto-Sleepers, an early user of the new Commer van.

The start of the decade saw more folk use there campervans abroad, travelling through Europe and beyond. Press reports further reinforced the campervan's advantages over, say, a touring caravan. With no towing or low speed limits, the campervan proved its worth for many, but with prices rising some manufacturers offered the customer the chance to buy a used van and then have the converter do a new conversion. This practice is still in evidence in modern times and for those wanting the latest interior design, this can be an ideal way to keep costs down. The idea was to prove a popular one for campervan buyers.

This decade also witnessed the spread of campervan dealerships. VW dealerships also began selling VW-based conversions by Devon and Danbury, which had official VW approval because the converters didn't alter anything that might affect the strength of the unit. VW was keen on campervan custom and one of their dealers,

Above left: This self conversion looks to have been carried out to a good standard. Holdsworth Campervans supplied DIY self-assembly furniture as a separate business.

Above right: Auto-Sleepers built up a reputation for quality design and furniture finish, as seen in this 1969 Commer conversion.

Right: The campervan sold to many because of its image as a versatile vehicle for everyday use. These promotional photographs show this to good effect.

Below: VW was a favourite base, but few had their approval for converting. Devon was one of the companies that did, with their 1965/1966 models seen here.

Service Garages of Colchester, a VW dealership, wanted to prove how a VW-based Devon Caravette could cover a large distance in comfort and economically. To achieve this they took the vehicle on a whistle-stop tour of the country. Note the Esso 3-star fuel used for the run.

Service Garages of Colchester, was sponsored by Esso and the Auto Camping Club in 1969. The idea was to stage a driving event while keeping to all the speed limits and with a straight-out-of-the-showroom Devon Caravette with 9,000 miles on the clock. The ensuing marathon around the UK covered 2,460 miles and took just over sixty-five hours, only making stops for fuel. The Devon had an extra fuel tank, which helped reduce the number of stops required. The starting point was the Colchester-based garage, and from here the local mayor saw the team off, along with press and a bit of a party complete with balloons. The idea was to show just how economically you could tour the whole of the country and with ease. The four-man team took turns driving and one member said, 'We lived off soup and coffee the whole trip', and that eating on the move was also not an easy task. The exercise had seen the Devon on motorways, down back lanes and on some very exposed roads in bad weather. The whole project had been the brainchild of John Morgan, the sales manager of Service Garages, and soon he had Devon on board with the idea. In a time of limited coverage, it proved to be a good PR event for the garage and the campervan movement.

By the mid-1960s the Motor Caravanners Club was thriving and staged rallies around the UK, members forming long-term friendships. Dealers were present at some of the larger events and made a few sales in the process. The 1960s also saw great progress as the small

Above: The endurance run carries on – and the participants are still dressing as salesmen with ties worn. All in a day's work!

Right: Seen parked outside the Land's End Hotel, this endurance run created good publicity for the campervan lifestyle.

delivery van market expanded further with the launch of the first new Commer van in 1960. This new van under the Rootes Group boasted a 1500-cc engine with a 54-bhp output, but Rootes also gave the Commer FC buyer a diesel option. This was a Perkins 1600 cc engine with 42 bhp and claimed excellent fuel economy. With no turbo, it was a sluggish engine, though it proved to be durable.

Many converters saw the advantage of the new Commer, it being larger than a Ford Thames. This 763-kg vehicle was wider, allowing converters to add a transverse bed, and soon won over more converters with Auto-Sleepers making a very successful conversion

Above: The lightweight delivery-van revolution saw the launch of the then Rootes Group's new Commer. Larger than the Thames, it allowed for different layouts.

Left: Rootes gave their Commer van two engine options, although the diesel version would only account for a small proportion of its sales.

using it. Commer even did their own conversion as well as supplying other converters and motorhome manufacturers. Bluebird, a large caravan manufacturer, had stepped into motorhome manufacturing in late 1957 with a coach-built model known as the Highwayman.

By 1963 the company had merged with Sprite & Eccles Caravans, a fast-expanding manufacturing group. The merger witnessed the establishment of a new group company, named Caravans International (CI) (see the author's book *The Story of Caravans International* (Amberley Publishing, 2017)). Bluebird launched the Moto Plus, a conversion based on the Austin and Morris J4 van. Costing £795, it was classed as a car/caravan and was fully insulated and had polished Limba-ply interior walls. They also launched the Wayfarer, available on the Commer and J4, in the early 1960s. Both campervans were sold under the Bluebird badge along with the coach-built Bluebird Highwayman.

The new CI group expanded its empire by taking in several other manufacturers, including German maker Wilk-Stern. CI became the world's largest leisure-vehicle manufacturer, producing tourers, holiday homes, mobile homes, motorhomes and

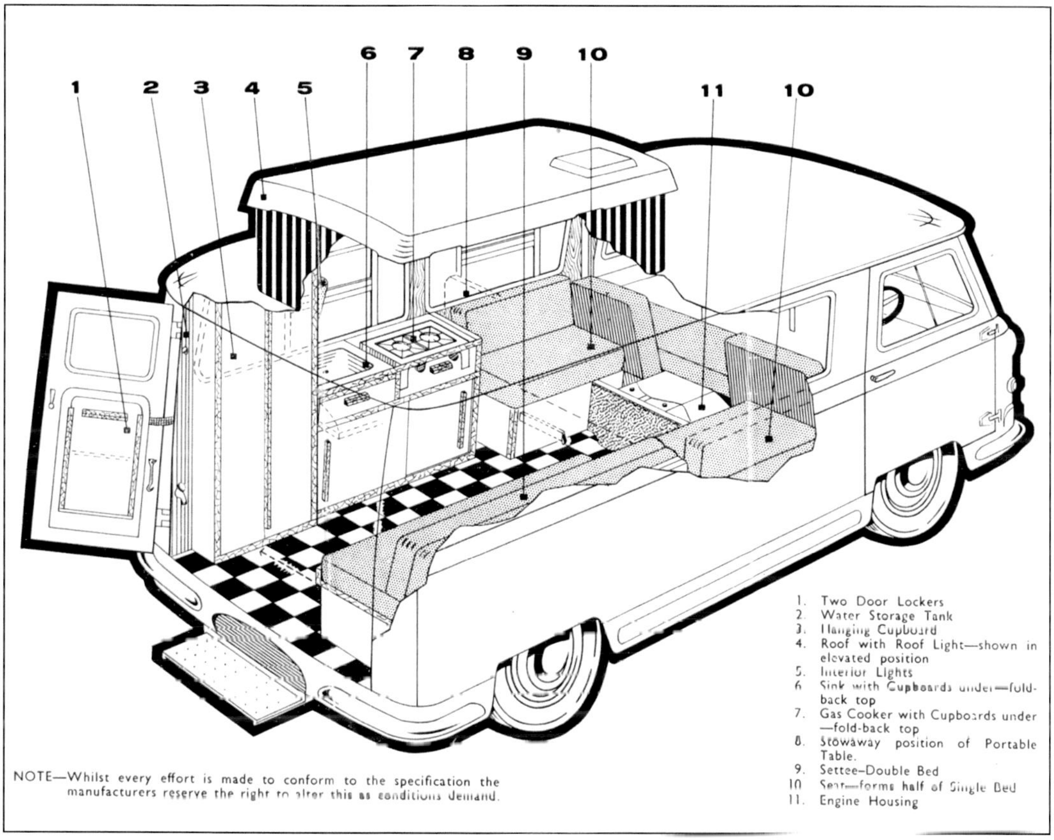

Caravan manufacturer Bluebird began producing motorhomes in 1958. A few years later it introduced its Morris/Austin campervan, the Moto Plus, which cost £795.

Above: Bluebird used the recently launched Rootes Commer van for their Wayfarer campervan conversion in 1964.

Left: In 1963 the Bluebird name was dropped from its campervans and motorhomes and instead came under Caravans International Motorised, a new division within the ever-expanding CI Group.

campervans and expanding with factories in South Africa, Italy, Germany, France, Sweden, New Zealand and the US. By 1966 a new division had been set up and was responsible for the motorised caravan division. CIM (Caravans International Motorised) essentially saw part of the Bluebird caravan factory at Poole specialise in motorhomes and conversions based initially on the Ford Thames. However, with the Commer, CIM allowed their designers more room to deliver a spacious and practical layout.

By 1971 CI had rebranded its expanding campervan/motorhome division as Autohomes, a name that was to become well known all over Europe with many models being exported. The CI Group dominated the global market from the late 1960s to the end of the 1970s. Overall, all campervans were becoming better specified from the early half of the 1960s with onboard water tank, oven/cooker/grill, gas and 12-V lighting and pumped water to the sink. A couple of manufacturers fitted a fridge as standard, which ran on gas, ideal if touring abroad, of course, but most had a cool box or lightweight portable fridge such as the Axim Cara-Frig.

The attraction of owning or hiring a campervan was that it was seen to be ideal for children by those parents who could afford £800-plus for a new or second-hand example.

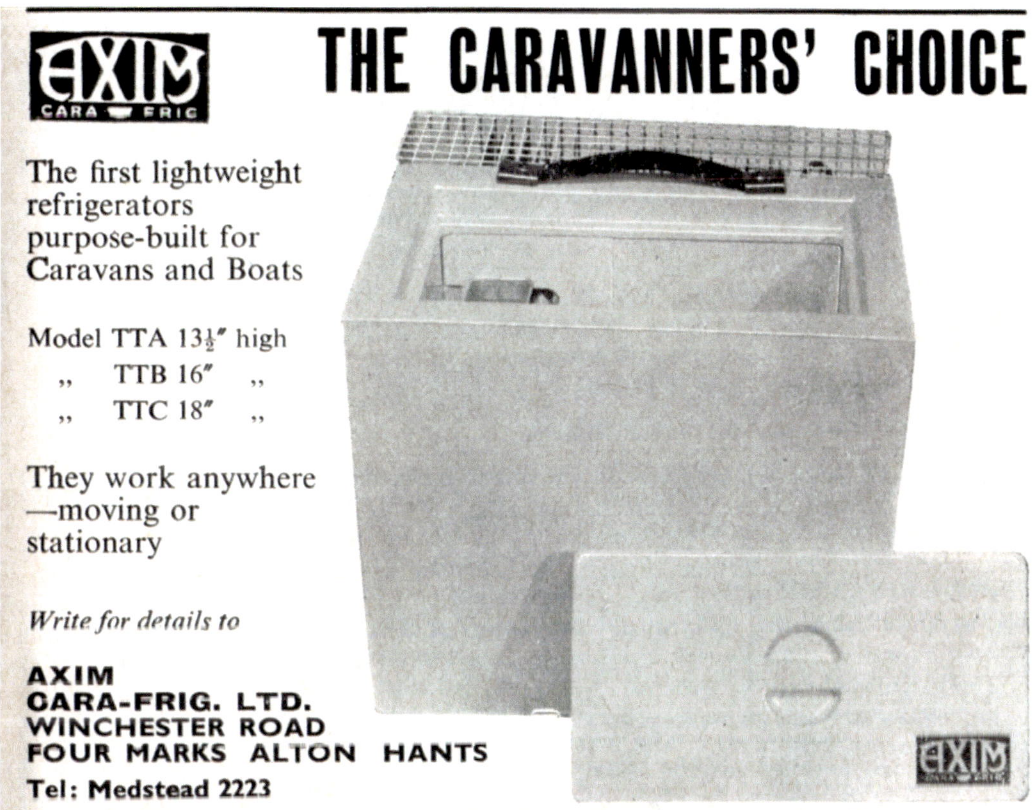

For some, fridges were more affordable for their campervan than a cool box. The Cara-Frig was not a great brand name.

Above: The campervan lifestyle was seen as a way of experiencing true freedom – hence families loved it, as this image shows.

Left: Increasing sales saw the emergence of new campervan dealers. Wilson's, which entered the market early on, had an impressive showroom on Acre Lane in London.

The fact that the campervan could be used for everyday transport and days out as well as a last-minute getaways sold the idea to a growing number of buyers. Many campervan users had started with a tent and had progressed to caravans, but for some the campervan meant no towing or even a change of the family car. Danbury was one of many new converters being established and soon built a loyal following.

Above: By the late 1960s more and more campervans were being seen. This family show how self-contained they are with a campervan – you can almost see them gloating as the family in the car make do.

Right: Danbury used VW and became a brand favourite after being established in Essex in 1964. This advert emphasises 'forward facing seats' as a feature.

Above: Even a day out in a campervan felt like a mini-break, although it is extremely unlikely that you can take your campervan down to the beach now as they did in 1968.

Left: Where next, dad? In the 1960s there were fewer restrictions and fenced-off beauty spots, as this family demonstrates.

Back then it was still easy to pull into a small road and find a place to park up for a night or stop on a beach with few restrictions. These days most pull-ins like that are now fenced off and overnight stays are prohibited. Families were portrayed using campervans and most layouts offered bunks in the high-top or elevating roof, while mum and dad had the double bed below. Gas bottles were stored in a dedicated compartment and beds were more comfortable than in the early days. Vehicle specifications were changing rapidly and electric mains became available, although sites with electrics were still scarce. Making more space within and adjoining a campervan could be achieved in various ways, from an attached awning to a separate side awning/tent, a trend that has become popular again in more recent times.

The campervan conversion boom would be further helped when in 1965 Ford launched a new van. Originally named the Thames, it was changed to Transit, a name that would become well known outside of the UK too. The new Transit was a significant move away from the Thames. The Transit was larger and had a car-like bonnet with easy access to the engine. The Transit being larger, it offered more storage and went on to be available in various forms over the coming years. The Transit was a gift to converters with Car Camper,

Space was something campervan users needed and tent and caravan awning makers came up with attached and lean-to designs, as seen here.

Left: A side and rear attachment design by Invader, the Vanex was available in several bright colours in the late 1960s.

Below: Ford's Thames van was replaced with the bigger and better Transit in 1965. Easier to drive and service, Dormobile was the first to do a conversion with it.

Freedom and Dormobile being first to convert the Ford Transit, closely followed by other companies soon after. The Transit offered a reliable base for converters and was a massive improvement on the Ford Thames it replaced.

Commer also enhanced its van, adding a larger engine over 1700 cc. Now part of Chrysler, Commer had built their own campervan as well as supplying other makers. With rising

Above: Alongside other converters, Midlands-based newbie Car Camper was quick to grab the Transit to convert.

Below: In 1968 Coachwork Conversions produced the Freedom campervan using the Transit. Along with an elevating roof, it had a well-finished interior.

demand for CIM's coach-built Highwayman and helped by a £2 million order from the US, where the Highwayman was named the Sunbeam Funwagon, Chrysler needed to concentrate on supplying Commers to CIM and other converters. In late 1967 VW launched its new T2, dropping the split-screen design and making the popular campervan base more sought after by converters.

The VW was used by many converters and DIY folk and Dormobile had taken up the German van by 1962. The new Dormobile VW Kombi was priced at £915 and featured the specially designed Dormatic patented seats, which allowed for easy bed making and folded away into the side wall to free up more floor area for bulky items. By 1962/3 Dormobile had

The VW T2 was more attractive looking than the original split-screen version. In 1968 Canterbury was an early converter of the T2.

Devoted to Bedford, Dormobile did use the early VW split-screen in 1962, along with the Austin J4 and Ford Thames.

dropped the BMC J2 after adding the VW Kombi. Dormobile was now the biggest producer of campervans and had a large market share, their designs winning approval particularly as they chose popular vans to convert.

Small converters were starting to appear and this gave the campervan buyer an even larger selection of models to choose from. Names to come into the market that would go on to become well known were Richard Holdsworth and Sun-Tor, both established around 1968. Holdsworth was a husband-and-wife team who after converting a van were asked to convert another and soon a business was up and running, expanding after just a year. Holdsworth's conversions were sought after by buyers especially as they also produced furniture kits for DIY folk. The company grew and ventured into coach-built models too.

Sun-Tor began in Toddington, Devon, and took the Austin A55 half-ton BMC van and converted it to a campervan. The Sun-Tor is classed today as a micro-campervan, so essentially the same as the estate-car version of the A55 which was introduced in 1957. At the Earls Court Caravan Show in 1968 the two on the stand were sold within two days. The well-finished and cleverly planned Sun-Tor could accommodate up to four with two sleeping in the elevating roof. One other base vehicle that could easily be overlooked was the Renault Estafette used by Coachwork Conversions of Berkhamsted in 1962. It came

The 1962 VW-based Dormobile featured specially designed fold-away seats to create more space when not needed.

Founded in Devon in 1968, Torcars produced micro-campervans. The Austin A60 was a good seller for them with over 300 converted in four years.

with a good specification for its time, offering glasses, crockery, kettle, litterbin and gas cylinder as well as a rear porch awning. It could seat up to seven and the Renault looked to have potential as a campervan, although it had a fixed roof. No other companies took up the van and as a campervan it fell by the wayside in 1966.

Models converted Renault, Commer.

Seating Up to seven.

Berths Two adults, two children.

Doors Side and rear.

Fittings Wardrobe, lockers, cupboards, table, sink, cooker, nest of kitchen utensils, litter bin, curtains, crockery, cutlery, glassware, whistling kettle. Awning at rear. Gas cylinder.

Canopy Solid top.

Colour Single.

Price Renault £909. Commer £919.

Length 13′ 5½″
Height 6′ 3½″
Width 5′ 10″
} Renault

Weight 21 cwt.

Length 14′ 1″
Height 6′ 10″
Width 6′ 4″
} Commer Camper Coach

Weight 21 cwt.

A Seats into single berth
B Locker seat
C Table (converts with B to make double berth)
D Locker seat in single berth
E Gas cooker
F Basin
G Drawer with 6 gallon tank under
H Taps
I Clip on canvas screen over back doors

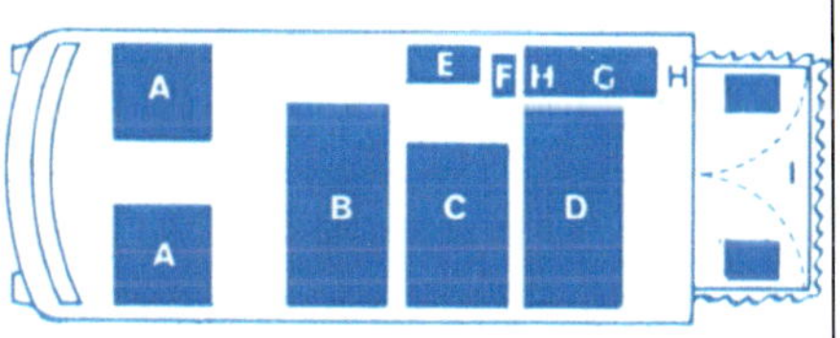

THE MOST COMPLETELY EQUIPPED MODEL ON THE MARKET

Renault

Touriste

From 1962 the Renault Estafette was converted by Coachwork Conversions, but there were few sold.

In recent times there has been a move towards 4 x 4 campervans, designed for those wanting to get more off the beaten track. However, this idea is nothing new and in the 1960s it was thought that some customers might want their campervans to get to places that other campervans couldn't get to. At this time there was only one truly versatile vehicle, and it was a true mountain goat of a vehicle – the Land Rover. There were those who wanted to go further afield and down tracks, but, of course, conventional campervans were not designed for such excursions. The Land Rover was the ideal vehicle but could it be converted? And if so, by whom?

In 1961 Martin-Walter would be the first to put the idea into practice, using a long-wheelbase version, the extra length providing space for the kitchen, which was unusually made from aluminium. The Dormobile Land Rover cost £1,198 and production would last for several years. R. J. Searle was another converter of the Land Rover, naming their product the Carawagon and undercutting the Dormobile at £1,180. Very much a niche market, no official sales figures were reported over the years and only a few remain in existence. Both Dormobile and Searle thought the Land Rover would sell better than it did, but sales were limited. Images of wild camping with the Land Rover Carawagon were used to promote the conversion. However, the campervan owner was now permitted to stop on most commercial and club sites with facilities and mainly chose these places to pitch for a few nights.

Land Rovers being converted at the Dormobile works during the mid-1960s. Most of these were sold abroad.

Right: Dormobile advertised the Land Rover conversion and had Land Rover's approval.

Below: The Carawagon by R. J. Searle. This converter also had their own Land Rover conversion and also used other vehicles as bases.

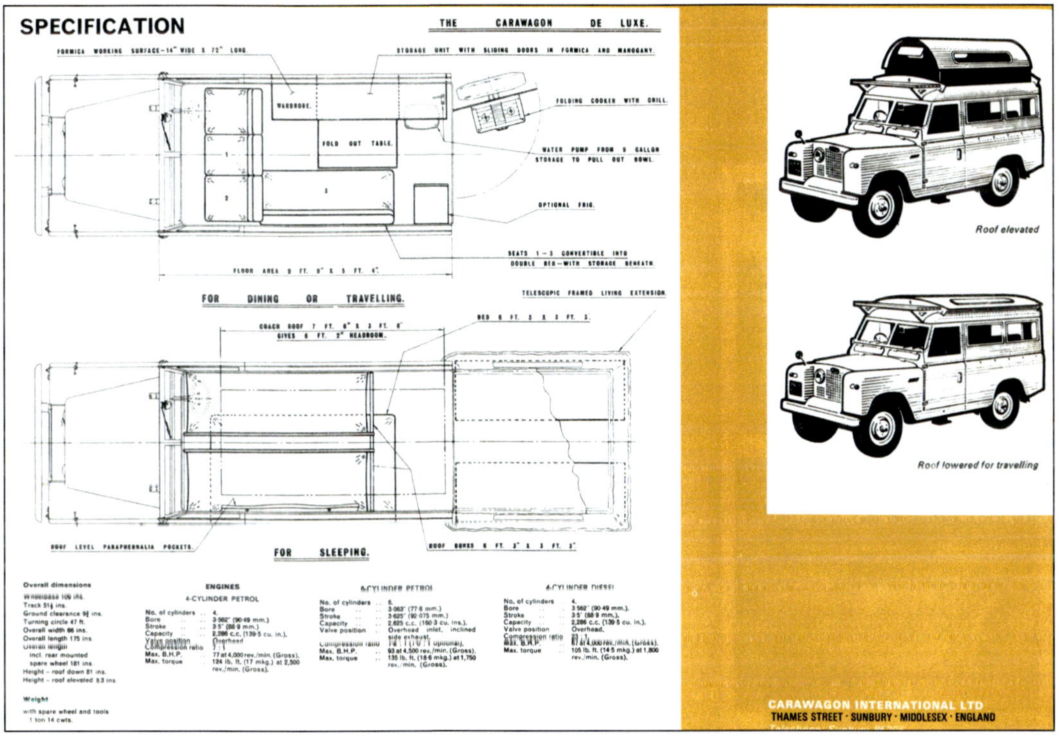

Left: A Carawagon PR shot showing that the Land Rover allowed real off-road camping, bringing adventure to campervan life!

Below: Roland and Leon Watts proving that a campervan adventure wasn't just for the fully abled person. They planned a 20,000-mile trip in their VW.

This decade witnessed the publication of a new magazine for campervan owners named *The Motor Caravan and Camping*, priced at 2*s* 6*d* (18p), which would become today's *MMM* magazine. It gave the campervan owner lots of tips and all the latest news and ideas for places to go touring. One news story worthy of mention from 1969 was that of two brothers, Roland and Leon Watts. Leon had been paralysed by polio at the age of thirteen and had an iron-lung machine he had to use twelve hours a day. The duo had planned a 20,000-mile trip in a VW T2, which would see them visit India. Thorough preparations were made for Leon, including a petrol generator and hand pump for his lung machine.

DIY features got readers doing jobs on their vans and fitting ovens and fridges – there were no health and safety regulations or Corgi-registered fitters then. Especially if taking their vans abroad, campervan owners were encouraged to join the AA Continental Touring service. Readers were also told how to maintain a campervan, checking springs and bodywork for rust, which was a major problem at this time. Rust traps were common on cars and also vans and no under sealing was routinely applied back then. There were various under-seal paints available and these could be applied by the user or a garage. However, most of these products were not very effective. Other treatments included spray wax, but the body joints would see paint flake, allowing rust to set in quickly. If you were buying a used van to have converted, it was strongly recommended that engine checks as well as body checks were carried out. At the time it was easy to fiddle with the mileage on a vehicle and clocking, as it was known, was rife. With the rise in interest in campervans and motorhomes, several books on the subject were published, such as *Motor Caravanning* by Tim Wilkinson in 1968, priced at 30*s* (£1.50). Books like this offered tips on buying and what you might require on tour, from cool boxes to medical supplies.

A number of books were written for the campervan and motorhome owner during this period. *Motor Caravanning* included all sorts of tips and advice.

The rising roof that allowed headroom on site was by this point available in many designs. Ironically, some manufacturers of campervans would use a rising roof from a competitor. There were several companies around supplying campervan converters with designs on a freelance basis, such as Spacemaker, Parkstone, Gentlelux, Weathershileds and Sherwood. Designs included the concertina style, as used by Dormobile, and the straight-up or folded-up style. Some were solid while others had material sides, some had a wooden structure and some were made of glass fibre. Many were supplied to DIY converters and the various designs all had their plusses as well as their minuses. Some considered Dormobile's concertina design the best, but there were many options to choose from.

With vehicle dealerships expanding, some took the plunge and began dealing solely in campervans, specialising in just a few makers and selling their products new. These dealers also began to offer campervan hiring as another way to get folk to try this leisure vehicle. Many dealers had a hire fleet, but it was Wilson's large car dealership that expanded its campervan and motorhome hire and sales business on an almost global scale. Wilson's were London-based and along with Turner's, another sizeable concern, these two led the

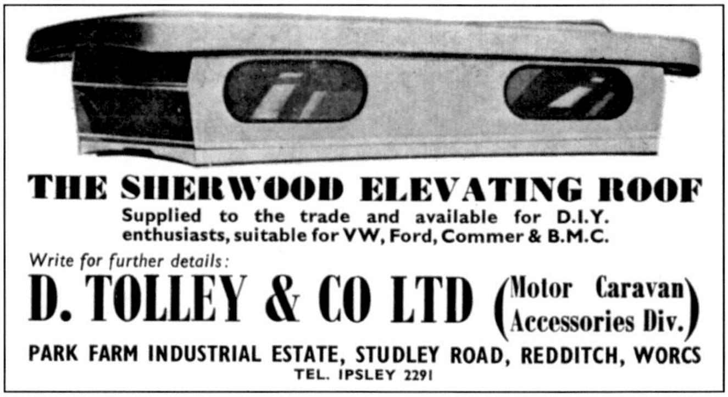

Above: The Sherwood, one of several elevating roofs that were manufactured and used by campervan converters and DIY folk. This was one of the most popular designs available.

Left: The interior of the Sun-Tor Austin A60 micro-campervan. This conversion was well planned and finished, with over 300 sold in six years.

way, Wilson's being the larger of the two. The campervan hire business was successful and with an ever-growing choice of models, there was something to suit most users' needs.

The micro-campervan was to come into play in the 1960s. Torcars' conversion of the BMC van, as mentioned above, fitted a quart into a pint pot, as it were. In 1967 Dormobile designed a campervan using the Bedford HA 8-cwt (407-kg) delivery van. This van was based on the Vauxhall Viva small family car and the designers at Dormobile had to make use of every inch of the van's interior space. Sleeping up to three, the Roma, as it was designated, included the now-famous, in campervan circles, rising roof with the traditional candy-stripe pattern. Internally there was a side dinette with kitchen opposite, including a fold-away sink, one-burner stove and grill and, although the kitchen was tiny, a 27-litre onboard fresh-water carrier.

The Roma with its 1200-cc engine would have proved to be a sedate drive, but back then life was at a slower pace and probably nobody noticed this. The Roma also had an optional-extra fold-away section at the rear for another bed. Classed as an all-round vehicle, it was also sold on its compactness and use as an everyday vehicle. Another car/ van that would be seen as an ideal micro-campervan was launched to the motoring public

In the 1960s Dormobile produced a micro-campervan using the Bedford HA 407-kg van, naming it the Roma. It had an extended rear end for the bed.

The Roma interior showing car mode and how it looks with the main double bed made up and the tiny furniture units.

in January 1968, the Ford Escort. The successor to the popular Ford Anglia, the Escort had modern styling. Estate and van versions helped boost sales further, making it a top seller in the UK. It also attracted several converters in the early part of the 1970s, which will be discussed in the next chapter.

VW campervans, popular as ever, had even by this early stage become iconic and many could be spotted in towns and car parks as well as travelling around the UK's roads. The familiar sound of the air-cooled VW engine was the telltale sign. By 1968 the T2 was out and looked more modern but still retained the distinctive VW design. As the 1960s drew to a close, Bedford's CF van was looking old in the tooth and with 370,000 produced, plans for a replacement were on the cards. Enter the Bedford CA, a new larger, more modern van that converters would be eager to add to their line-up. In 1969 this was the big news from Luton, and Dormobile would be first off the mark with Bedford giving them priority after the success of the CA conversions. CIM was also given priority and launched a new Bedford CF named the Brigand, with Auto-Sleepers and Canterbury using the CF too.

The new Bedford was larger and more car-like to drive and was mainly in competition with the Ford Transit, although it also proved to be a worthy alternative to the VW and the Commer for converters. Accessories became more prominent and this growing market saw campervan dealerships upgrade from small areas stocking essential items to full-blown

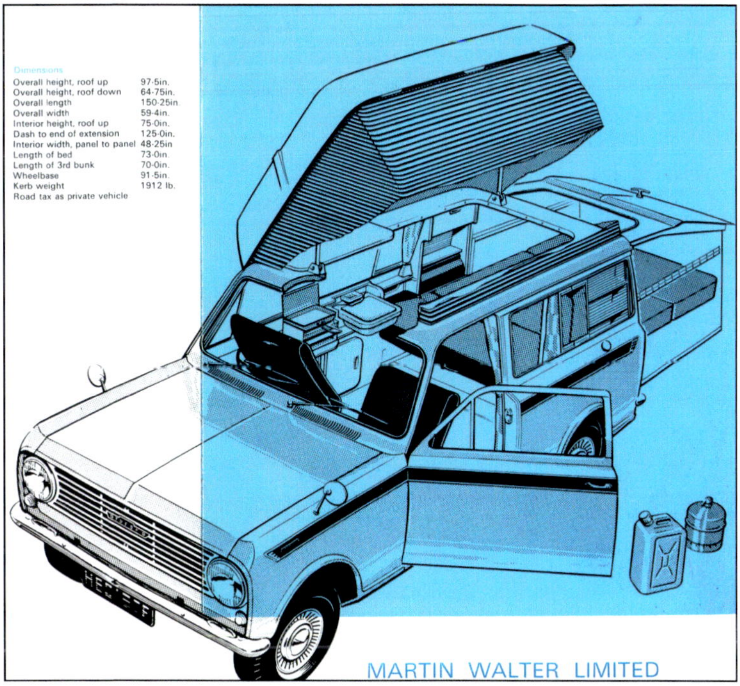

Right: An exploded view of the Roma micro-campervan, a clever design that sold quite well.

Below: Bedford's CA sold well and many were converted, mainly by Dormobile. However, as this 1966 image shows, it was starting to look dated.

Bedford launched its new CF in late 1969 and Dormobile was one of the first to convert it straight away along with CIM from Poole.

hanimex/toshiba portable tv

A NEW 11-inch monochrome portable TV set is available from Toshiba with advanced styling and appearance not normally associated with a small portable unit. Controls for channel selection, volume, contrast and brightness are located in a small and convenient space beside the picture tube. With a weight of less than $15\frac{1}{2}$-lb and a recommended retail price of £79 10s 0d the Toshiba 11TBB is produced specifically for British transmission on standard UHF channels 21-68. The set is transistorised, incorporating the latest TV technology and operates from either an ac (220-240V) or dc (12V) power source with a black-tinted screen and black filter to reduce glare and ensure "easy on the eyes" viewing both indoors and out.

An outdoor aerial socket as well as a loop antenna for inside use is incorporated. The set has a carrying handle and comes complete with an impact resistant polystyrene case.

The Toshiba 11TBB television set is available through leading radio and electrical shops and departmental stores.

Portable TVs such as this Toshiba 12-V/mains-operated unit were ideal for campervan use. The 11-inch screen was big enough in a tight space.

dedicated sales areas showing many more products, such as crockery especially designed for the campervan user. Campervan accessories mirrored those used by caravanners and commonly featured items such as Whale pumps, Electrolux fridges, portable TVs and Flavel ovens. The 1960s had also seen more campervan owners travelling abroad, resulting in an increased requirement for a fridge, an option that was progressively added to buyers' wish-lists.

The 1960s had seen the micro-campervan gain popularity, and in 1969 the micro Fiat 600T was used as a conversion by Motor Caravan Conversions Ltd. This car-like van was seen as the answer for holidays and weekends for a small family. The Fiat was reported to achieve over 45 mpg and enabled a small family to have a touring holiday in comfort. It was an extremely well-designed micro-campervan and in 1970 the engine size of 850 cc was increased to 900 cc, producing 33 BHP. The Fargo model from Motor Caravan Conversions sold well and the next decade would see sales increase as new models were added by the company. Ending on a high, by late 1969 campervan sales were around 4,000 units, a figure that would climb further in the early 1970s.

Above: Fiat's 600T van was an unlikely candidate for a conversion, but Motor Caravan Conversions took on the challenge, naming it Fargo.

Right: The Fargo was a true micro-campervan. MCC did a practical conversion and set a new benchmark in micro-campervan design.

3

THE 1970S – A NEW ERA OF THE CAMPERVAN

The 1970s began as a decade of hope but then took a gloomy turn as the economy dived and inflation hit 24 per cent, the oil crisis loomed and the three-day week was introduced. There were petrol shortages with fuel coupons issued, although they were never used, and a top speed limit of 50 mph was brought in. VAT was added to caravans, motorhomes and campervans for the first time. There were mixed fortunes for the UK leisure-vehicle industry to say the least. However, the start of the 1970s would see a bigger increase in campervan sales as well as motorhomes. Dormobile had a national TV advert, although personally I can't remember it, but I was only ten at the time! Dormobile began to use computers in production schedules, while Peter Pitt, the brainchild behind the UK campervan, had sadly died and in reduced circumstances despite his success in the industry.

The boom in motorhome and campervan sales saw them take a bigger slice of the vehicle market with 7,000 units produced and sold in the UK. New converters came and went. Creighton converted the latest Bedford CF in 1972, naming it the Clubman, which featured their own elevating-roof design. The Caravan and Camping Show at Earls Court saw more converters displaying the latest in campervans. Auto-Sleepers would take large stand space along with Dormobile and Danbury. Shows were vital to campervan

The Creighton Clubman Bedford-based campervan, *c.* 1972. Based in Nelson, Lancashire, this manufacturer of caravans and boats was small, so production numbers were limited.

makers who attended both local events and larger national ones, such as the Scottish Caravan Show and the Colex Show. Dealers would also use their showrooms to stage special weekend sales events, especially in the early part of the year or towards the end of it. With complimentary refreshments on offer and promotional adverts in the local press, these were often well attended and good sales achieved. With such demand for

Above: The Auto-Sleepers stand at the Earls Court show, *c*. 1973. This was one of several shows that allowed campervans to be seen by a wider audience.

Right: The Danbury campervan stand at Earls Court Olympia, a show that was always busy.

Holiday in Transit '71

Above: Madison's had been car dealers and had moved into campervans by 1971. Here prospective customers are attending the opening night in the Madison showroom in November of that year.

Left: Meet the team! Car dealerships began to get into the campervan retail area, especially in the early 1970s.

campervans, car dealerships sometimes moved to campervan sales only, making more profit on these than on cars.

Madison's Motors, based in Southport, had by 1970 begun selling campervans and in 1971 expanded its operation and started attending local shows. Madison's soon became well known in campervan circles for its choice of motorhomes and from 1972 attended the Earls Court Caravan and Camping Show at Olympia. The company expanded further and

Madison's display at Southport, 1973. Dormobile Romas, based on the Bedford/Vauxhall Viva, dominate the front row.

By 1973 Madison's had moved into new premises near Preston, Lancashire. This is their stand at the one-time Manchester Bell Vue event.

Madison's would grow at a rapid rate in the early 1970s, expanding and attending local caravan and camping shows.

by 1973 had moved into larger premises with a big indoor showroom on the outskirts of Blackpool. They went on to produce their own magazine and organise Madison's customer campervan rallies. In 1973 Madison's opened a new large showroom and showground on the outskirts of Preston. Several celebrities of the day visited, including comedian Charlie Chester, who opened the new premises in March 1973. Fellow comedian Ken Dodd also made a trip to the new showroom in 1975, using his experience as the basis for a TV sketch. Madison's sold Burmah petrol and was awarded a prize by the oil company which was presented by Jimmy Tarbuck. Madison's became a magnet for stars at the various industry shows, such as the 1974 Earls Court event when 'Carry On' stars Sid James and Barbara Windsor were snapped in a campervan with Madison's finance director, Russell Lunt, on their stand.

Wilson's motorhome centre in Acre Lane, London, was one of the best retail showcases for campervans and motorhomes. The site is now home to a British Heart Foundation shop and there is little evidence of how it looked in its glory days.

Dormobile was still the biggest and most well-known campervan manufacturer, its factory in full production with large orders taken for its models. CIM, on the other hand, had seen demand for its models drop and it was decided to rebrand the campervan/

Prolific in PR, Madison's John Lunt shares a publicity shot with 'Carry On' stars Sid James and Barbara Windsor, *c.* 1973.

motorhome division. In 1971 CIM was to be rebranded as CI Autohomes for its coach-built models with a new, modern range of coach-builds available on several van chassis cabs, such as Ford and Commer. With expanding sales, the company had two premises, one for dispatching and the main factory on Ringwood Road, Poole. In 1973 a fourth production

Right: Wilson's was the biggest dealership at the time this photograph was taken in 1974. They had four showrooms, the most impressive site located at 36 Acre Lane, London.

Below: The CI Motorised division factory at 59 Wareham Road, Poole, 1973. Note the stock vans for conversion/coach-built motorhomes. They had another premises down the road.

line was implemented which added a new factory extension. Making CI's Autohomes' plant as big as Dormobile's, it now claimed to be the biggest UK maker of campervans and motorhomes. The campervan side was still known as CI – Motorised until 1973.

New converters emerged and with over 7,000 campervans/motorhomes sold in 1972, the market was definitely booming. With more leisure shows around, campervans were often exhibited. Once such event was the Miss Motor Caravan beauty pageant held at the Earls Court Olympia show in November 1974. The British Caravan Road Rally event also allowed campervans to participate, with a separate class for them. Caravans were raced around a track and there was also an off-road rallying competition, which were all good fun but had been dropped by the late 1970s.

Left: The Toyota Hi Ace vans production line at CI Motorised, 1973. These vehicles are being converted to campers.

Below: An advert and entry form for the Miss Motor Caravan 1975 contest.

MISS MOTOR CARAVAN 1975 BEAUTY CONTEST

Don't miss this chance to become Miss Motor Caravan and win a continental holiday for 2 and cash prizes.

CLOSING DATE EXTENDED TO 7TH DECEMBER

ALSO

Automatic entry for the finals of Miss Camping 1975 to be judged at Camping Outdoor Life Exhibition Olympia London in January. The last winner of this competition went on to become Miss World.

COMPETITION RULES

Competitors have to be *single* and aged between 18 and 25 on 1 July 1974.
Any Competitor who has previously represented England, Ireland, Wales or Scotland in any International Beauty Contest is ineligible.
Entry will be by photograph only, and our Finalists will parade in sweaters and shorts and in one-piece swimsuits, for the title of Miss Camping 1975 and a further prize of £250.
The organisers reserve the right to use any photographs taken.
All entrants must have had at least one weeks camping holiday.

To: Motor Caravan + Camping (Comp)
17/18 Henrietta Street, London.

Name ....

Address ....

....

....

Photograph enclosed

Vital Statistics: Bust .... Waist .... Hips ....

Above left: Dormobile's Ford Escort-based campervan named the Elba had moderate success, especially during the fuel crisis of 1973–74.

Above right: Canterbury also did a campervan version of the Ford Escort named the Siesta. The extension annex available for it is seen here.

The Ford Escort, which had taken the small family car market by storm and had also seen van and estate versions sell well, was perfect for a micro-campervan conversion. Dormobile, being experienced in this field with the Land Rover and Bedford HD van, saw the Escort estate as ideal for conversion, employing a rear extension, as used on the Bedford. Named the Elba, the new Dormobile model came into its own a year or two later during an economic downturn, a period of high inflation and petrol shortages. The Elba, though, was joined by Canterbury and its Ford Escort version named the Siesta, which cost around £1,200 in 1972 and sold well. North Devon-based Sun-Tor also did an Escort-based conversion.

The Siesta had the same basic design features as the Dormobile Elba, with side kitchen, cooker, sink and an onboard water tank. The 1300-cc engine was the power plant, as used in the 407-kg weight model. The Sun-Tor company went on to make a coach built model on a Leyland Sherpa and also the Morris Marina van, a conversion available by the early 1970s. The BMC A60 van that Sun-Tor used was discontinued in 1970, so a replacement was needed and the more modern Marina fitted the criteria. The Marina conversion by Sun-Tor proved a steady seller for a micro-campervan through the 1970s. Sun-Tor, though, would become owned by the Midlands dealership Brownhill's in 1979, after which the company ceased trading. The Marina was changed to the Morris Ital, with some conversions made before the company was wound down.

Sun-Tor used the newly launched Morris Marina van for its micro-campervan. This went on to become a successful model for them for over a decade.

Sun-Tor moved to a new factory and the old site was taken over by two ex-employees (C&W Conversions), who produced the Nimbus Escort-based campervans in 1973.

One of the new makers to appear in the 1970s was Nimbus (C&W) Conversions, which was established by ex-Sun-Tor employees. The company took over the old Sun-Tor works and used the Transit and Bedford CF, although they began with the Ford Escort. With 15,000 campervans/motorhome sold in 1973, the future of the campervan looked bright, but dark clouds on the horizon would see the leisure-vehicle market badly hit. The oil crisis that began in 1973 saw petrol in short supply and price rises. With the national miners' strike triggering the three-day week, VAT being introduced in April 1973 and inflation soaring, caravan and campervan/motorhome sales were badly affected into 1974 and 1975. Some dealers promoted the campervan as a cheaper way to holiday and dealer Godfrey Davis held a small promotional tour of nearby towns with caravans and campervans.

Right: Dealers such as the Godfrey Davis Group promoted the caravan and campervan side of the business with PR stunts, as shown in this image from 1974.

Below: MCC launched the Fiat-based Farina, a successful micro-campervan. Fiats had an issue with rust, so few survive today.

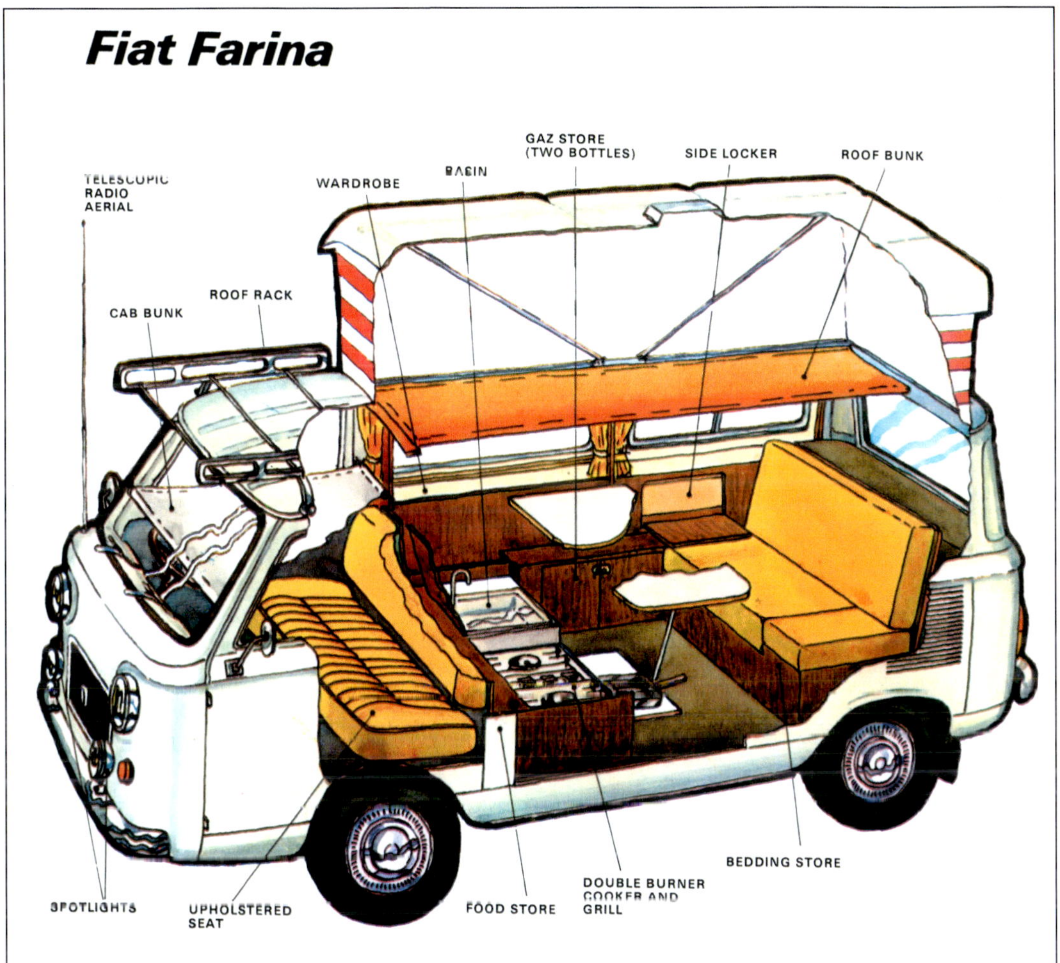

Motorhome sales would take more of a hit, but surprisingly campervan sales less so. However, demand for the micro-campervan was on the rise, and with Fiat increasing the engine size of its micro-van the 850T, converter Motor Caravan Conversions expanded its portfolio, adding the Farina model to its Fargo micro-campervan range. These micro-campervans came with rear extensions and elevating roofs and included family models. Back in 1973, I remember a brand-new 850T appearing in the school car park – it was a micro-campervan conversion. It belonged to the sports and maths teacher who was around 6 feet tall and had two children. I often wondered how they all fitted in, but he wasn't the sort of chap to ask questions about his vehicle. However, other teachers were heard teasing him about how a shoehorn could be useful to get them all in!

The Fiat campervan sold well and Dormobile saw the potential as fuel shortages and rising costs saw drivers ditch larger cars. Dormobile then produced their own conversion on the Fiat micro-campervan, but it wasn't as successful as MCC's, which came in several versions. Although the crises of the 1970s eased, campervan sales were far fewer than at the start of the decade. New base vans were still being launched, one being the Toyota Hi-Ace in 1972. This new model from Japan boasted features such as tinted glass and radios and it proved good for conversions. CI Motorised were first to use the Hi Ace, naming their model

Austerity campervan life in the mid-1970s – you will have a good time, kids!

Above: The CI Motorised Toyota Hi-Ace camper from 1974. The fridge was optional and the cooker pulled out for use.

Right: The Toyota Hi-Ace became a popular conversion with many campervan firms. This is Danbury's from 1975.

the Camper and this was a great success. Toyota wanted a slice of the VW market, and soon other converters such as Dormobile and Danbury would pick the 1.6 petrol-engine Toyota. VW shocked the campervan world when it stated that it would only supply converters that VW approved of. This left only Devon Campervans being eligible for using the VW Transporter for converting. By 1978 Devon had expanded its range with the Moonraker and Sundowner models.

With Rootes selling out to Chrysler, the Commer would now become the Dodge and receive updates, although it had become less popular by the late 1970s. Bedford and Ford would update to larger engines for the CF and Transit. One poor contender was BMC, now named Leyland. With old designs, sales fell fast and a new van was needed. Bringing in the

At one stage Devon was the only campervan converter to gain the approval of VW itself.

Auto-Sleepers produced luxury campervans and by 1973 was known for its quality. They started with Commer but moved to Bedford and then the Leyland Sherpa.

ex-Ford Transit designer, by 1974 the Leyland van had been launched, named the Sherpa a year later. This new British van was to prove popular with converters. Auto-Sleepers and Holdsworth were keen to bring this new base into their ranges but the Transit was still a popular choice.

With several converters having gone out of business, new ones began appearing. One of these was the Manchester Motor Caravan Company which produced high-tops as well as elevating roofs. The company had begun in late 1969 but didn't really get going until the 1970s. It produced DIY kits and sold the extending roofs to the DIY market. In the

Right: Canterbury used various vans but was one of the first to use the new Leyland Sherpa for its Sunseeker model in 1974.

Below: Holdsworth used VWs, Bedford and Ford's Transit, as seen here. Holdsworth founder Richard eventually went to work for Auto-Sleepers.

1980s the company became Leisuredrive, now one of the longest-established firms in the business. By the mid-1970s Devon had received large export orders from a French buyer but in the UK sales were around 6,000 despite predictions of 22,000 units. CI announced sales had dropped and its Poole plant laid off 200 staff in a bid to protect other jobs at the factory.

The situation would improve but the boom days were over, although the campervan market was still moving, just a lot more slowly. The idea of a tent extension or stand-alone tent for campervan users had been around since the early 1960s. The 1970s would see more modern and better designs with new imported makes such as Isabella, which grew its caravan-awning market share in the 1970s. Established in the UK in 1970, by the early part of the decade it had entered the campervan market and was firmly established by the late 1970s. Harrison was another well-known caravan-awning maker that was contributing new designs to the expanding campervan-annex tent market by the early 1970s.

Although sales had dropped to around 3,900 units, new models were still being launched. The Spacemaker Group expanded its ranges and brands and was at this point in the top three campervan producers alongside Dormobile and CIM, although CIM had become incorporated as CI Autohomes by the late 1970s. Other makers included Motorhomes International, Motor Caravan Conversions, Motorsleepers, Hilton Motorhomes and Viking Motorhomes, all of which produced campervans that used the Spacemaker-designed rising roof. Buccaneers were luxury campervans using the Bedford CF, Ford Transit, Commer and the Sherpa.

Above left: Carahome was a brand by Manchester Motor Caravans, which also made high-tops and furniture kits for DIY converters. By the early 1980s the company had become Leisuredrive.

Above right: Isabella, now a well-known awning manufacturer, only began importing to the UK in 1970. It soon established itself with campervan awnings and tent annexes.

Right: In 1972 Harrison, a UK manufacturer of caravan awnings, moved into campervan tents as well.

Below: The Buccaneer luxury campervan by Spacemaker. Another sizable concern, the company had several different brands by the mid-1970s.

The VW Transporter was a firm favourite as a base vehicle, and VW back-up service saw the introduction of computer diagnostics at VW service centres in 1973. This enabled quicker fault finding and was ahead of its time in 1973. Meanwhile, the Carawagon Land Rover-based campervan was given improvements and Searle saw the launch of the Range Rover as another conversion, making it a superior vehicle and describing the conversion as having deluxe touches. Mercedes launched a luxury high-top campervan in the mid-1970s, the Ultra Autobahn. This used the L106D base van and came with a 2.2 diesel engine as used in several Mercedes cars. The Autobahn had a high spec including shower, toilet, full oven and convector gas heater. Now a rare classic, it was a sign of imported campervans penetrating the UK market.

The 1970s had begun on a high but the ensuing economic crisis hit the industry hard, with sales crashing. By the end of the decade sales had recovered slightly and with new base vehicles on the horizon and imported campervans making inroads, there was still plenty happening. The 1980s would prove unpredictable with some names disappearing as a recession began to bite. The 1970s saw the campervan firmly put on the map and improved specifications, including items such as fridges, hot water, flushing toilets, showers, better 12-V lighting and heating, and ovens, gave this leisure vehicle even more kudos.

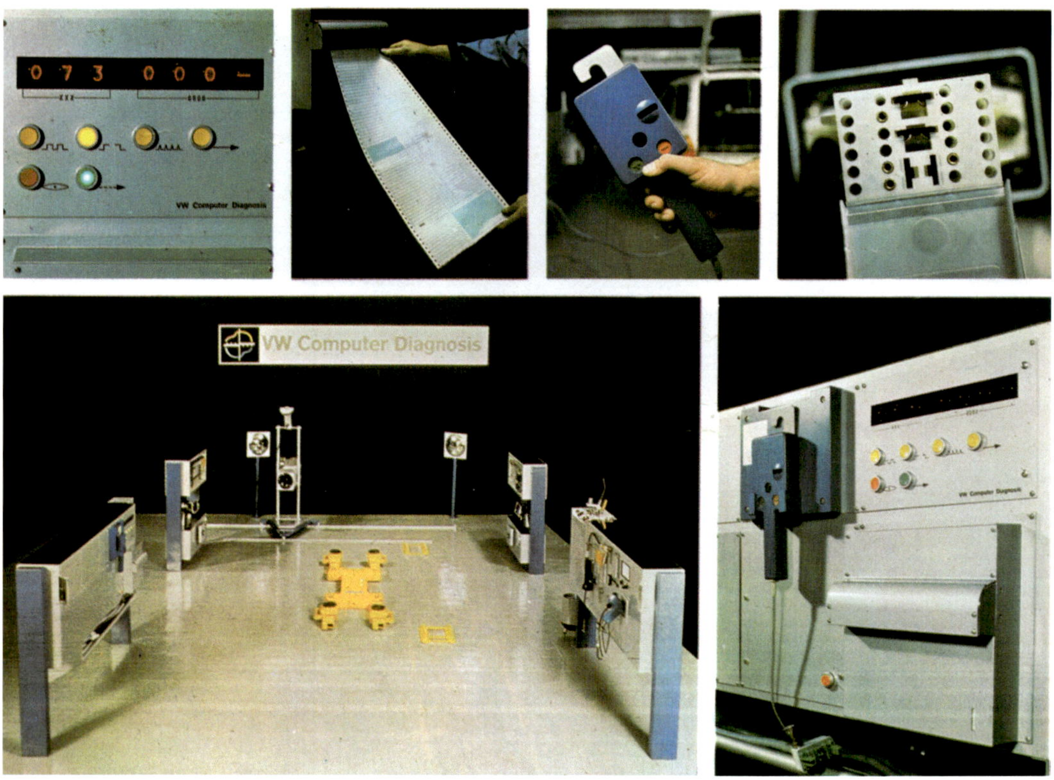

In the 1970s VW campervan owners could get faults sorted more quickly with the VW computer diagnostics machine.

Right: The Range Rover was a conversion from Carawagon. It was a luxury campervan with fridge, heater, etc., but sales were badly affected by the oil crisis between 1973 and 1974.

Below: The Mercedes Ultra Autobahn was launched in the mid-1970s. It was an early imported campervan but only available with a diesel engine.

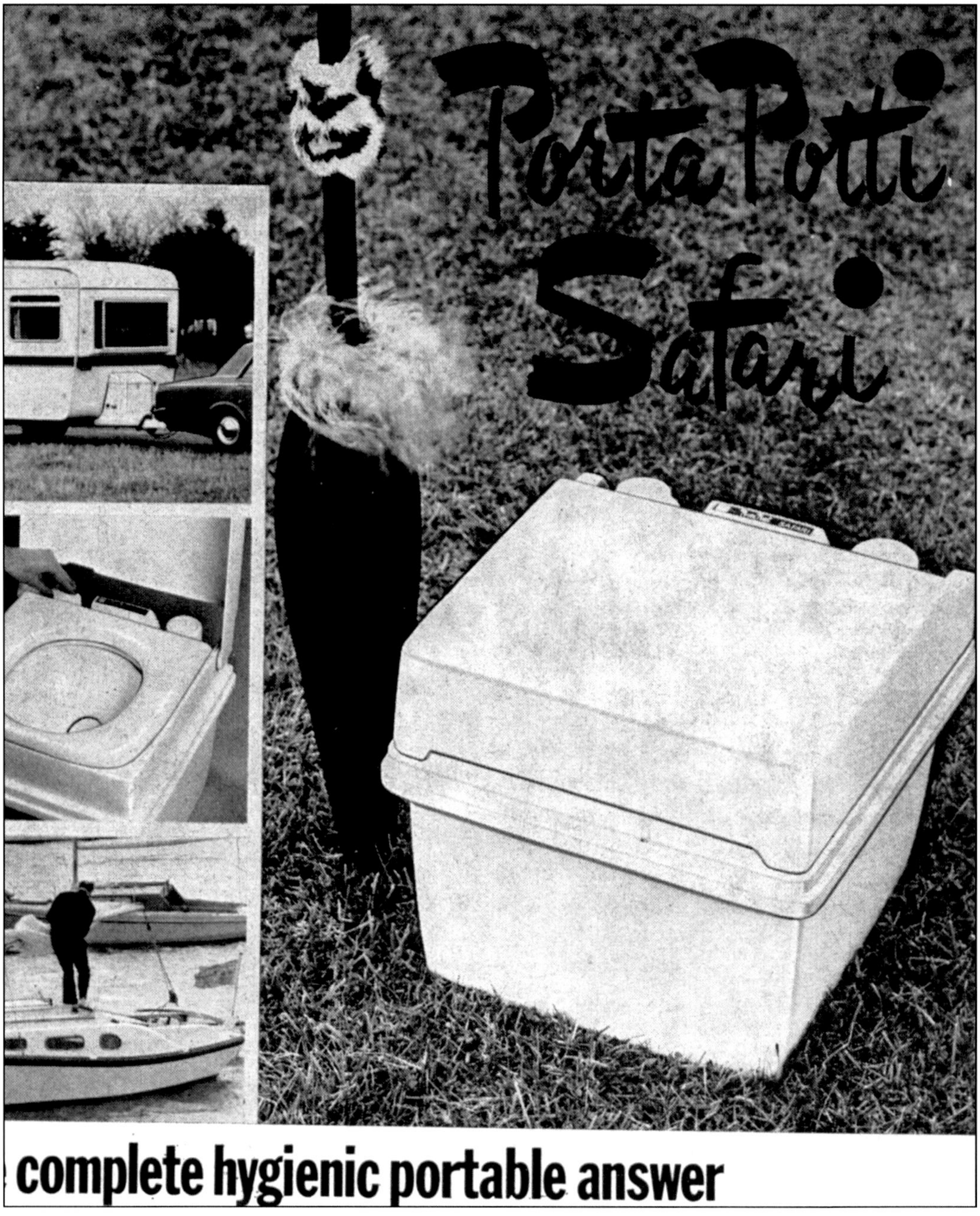

A greater range of accessories became available for the campervan user. Toilets were more compact than in the 1960s and could be stowed in smaller cupboards.

4

THE CAMPERVAN FROM 1980 TO THE PRESENT – UNEXPECTED TWISTS AND TURNS

The 1970s had been both a successful and disastrous decade for the campervan market. The 1980s proved to be another low decade with a high midway through. Names such as Car Camper, Canterbury, Motor Caravan Conversions, Haylett and York fell away. The recession in the early part of the decade saw sales slow in the leisure-vehicle market. However, this didn't stop new dealers such as Todd's Motorhomes coming into being and small concerns

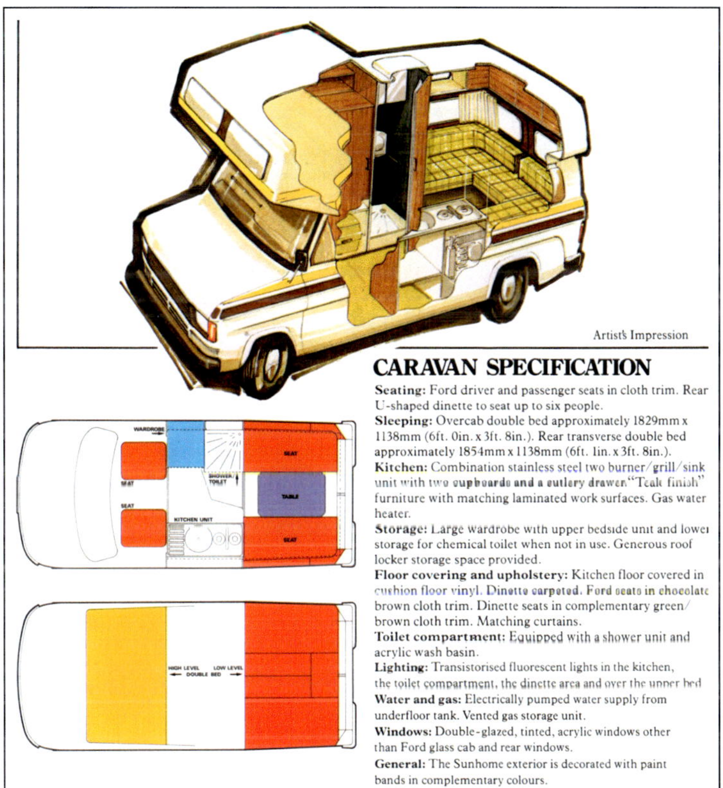

Canterbury's Ford Transit-based Sunhome with its unusual GRP moulded high top. The designers wanted to create a coach-built layout in a campervan.

Marquis began as a small concern in 1973, joining the then expanding network of campervan dealerships. This image shows the Lower Upham branch, near Southampton, one of twelve in the UK.

from the early 1970s such as Marquis expanding from one branch to several. Conversely, some of the early campervan dealers that had been successful, such as Turner's and the massive Wilson's, changed course and came out of the industry. Wilson's remains in business as a car dealership.

The mighty CI Group was also showing signs of problems with the Autohomes factory in Poole down to a one-day week in 1981. However, one model they thought of as a saviour was the Fiat 900E micro-campervan, aptly named Pandora with an extending elevating roof. Launched at the 1981 Earls Court Caravan Show, it generated lots of interest and was to be a good seller but all too late, unfortunately. Autohomes UK carried on with the Pandora until Fiat stopped production.

Dealerships carried out heavy discounting and sales drives to move stock. During this period many campervan dealerships would close, some of which were larger concerns, but as they did so, smaller dealers set up. With news of the CI Group collapse in late 1982, a reborn Autohomes UK under old hand Ian McPherson would see a new set of ideas and vehicle bases used bringing success to the reformed Autohomes. It mainly converted VW Transporters but also Bedfords, including the 1985 Midi. Named

Above left: The Autohomes Pandora micro-Fiat 900E was launched by the CI parent group, but was continued by the reformed Autohomes UK. This is the 1984 version with its roof extension erected.

Above right: From the ashes of CI Autohomes emerged Autohomes UK in 1983. It set about producing new models such as the Bedford Midi-based Midihome. With a high specification, this was launched in 1986 with a price tag of £11,495, but was only made for one season.

Autohomes' Komet VW-based four-berth high-top was launched in 1986. It went on to become one of Autohomes' top sellers in the UK.

the Midihome, the new Autohomes model was finished in silver, had a 1.8 petrol engine and an extensive specification, including blown air heating, toilet and mains electrics. Autohomes UK went on to launch new top-selling models such as the Kamper and Komet in conversions, which saw the company's fortunes pick up well by the mid-1980s.

The late 1980s would see more new versions of established delivery-van bases develop and caravan manufacturers such as Elddis and Swift turn to motorhomes and also venture into campervans. Cavalier Caravans in Felixstowe used the latest Bedford and launched its US-styled three-model campervan range. Unfortunately, it was not a success and by late 1981 the company had failed despite also converting a VWLT into a high-top version. Some of the older names such as Danbury and Devon would end up being taken over and

Elddis launched its Elegance Fiat Ducato-based campervan in 1988, the high-top being produced for several years. Elddis returned to campervans with its Fiat-based Autoquest CV range in 2019.

The interior of the Cavalier came with high specification and a US-themed interior. It may look somewhat outlandish now, but in the early 1980s it was the height of fashion!

Cavalier was a touring caravan brand but by 1980 had moved into campervans. Using Bedford as a base, it had its high-top roof placed at the rear and was greatly influenced by US design.

moving premises. Sun-Tor was bought out by Brownhill's but production of the Marina/Ital micro-campervan didn't last long.

Mains electric usually by Zig was being fitted by most campervan converters as sites geared up with mains-electric posts. Colour TVs became the norm, as did fridges fitted along with battery chargers and fresh-water tanks and waste tanks. Better insulation and plastic double-glazed windows became standard as users enjoyed their campervans into the colder months. Prices had risen over the years and with a price tag of £6,795 for a Ford-based Autohomes Trailblazer in 1981, this wasn't a cheap form of holidaying anymore. Petrol was £1 a gallon and this had an impact on sales, especially of older models. Diesel was introduced but it was not until engines had a turbo fitted and were more refined that this became a viable option for campervan owners. Devon campervans, though, bucked the trend with a luxury model called the Royalty, which featured a shower, large fridge, oven, mains, thermostatically controlled heating on a VWLT and cost £12,500, a substantial sum in 1980.

With the economy in a poor state, several small micro delivery vans from Suzuki, Honda, Bedford, Subaru, Daihatsu and Reliant came onto the market. These small-engine delivery vans took converters into another realm of design. Several took up the challenge, such as Danbury with its rear-end, full-width kitchen and sleeping two. The cost was just over £7,000 but £600 less with four wheel-drive not fitted. Danbury was the first to introduce the

Left: Devon was one of the early converters and bucked the trend with a luxury LT-based campervan, aptly named the Royalty.

Below: Danbury produced a Bedford Rascal micro-campervan named Renegade. It also used the Subaru 700 with 4 x 4 option which was named the Rogue, seen here.

autoroof

GREEN IS VWL.61H

THE DANBURY Volkswagen Series II is the first-ever motorised caravan to have an electrically-operated fully automatic elevating roof.

DANBURY brings you into the 1980's with modern technology – a combination of the best products from all countries, brought together by a BRITISH TEAM – a team which has styled the AUTOROOF to complement the advanced body design of the new Volkswagen Transporter – and, in so doing, has in no way impaired fuel economy, or detracted from the attractive lines of the vehicle.

This technically advanced integral part of the DANBURY, like all great ideas, is SIMPLICITY itself – effortless and reliable, it takes the hard work out of camping.

At the push of a button – the roof elevates SILENTLY – almost doubling the interior space – giving headroom for a giant, but operational by the smallest member of the family.

Danbury brought in the electric-operated elevating roof after the widow of the founder, Joy Dawson, struggled when she travelled alone in her campervan.

electric-operated elevating roof, after the wife of the founder, Joy Dawson, found it difficult to manually operate the elevating roof.

Renault launched its new Traffic van in 1980, offering a 2.1-litre diesel alongside its petrol options. Several converters used the Renault, Holdsworth and Auto-Sleepers being two, and although never a top choice, it went on to be widely used by other converters. The 4 x 4 idea for vans saw VW bring out a new design that enabled full four-wheel drive. In 1987 Renault added a 4 x 4 version to its Traffic line-up, but few converters took up this option of an all-terrain van. Fiat introduced its highly successful Ducato in 1982 and it became a popular conversion choice. The same was true of the Peugeot Boxer, although this didn't come into its own until 1993 when it was better presented and managed to carve out a share in the market. Others followed including Citroën's Relay. Converters were soon to exploit these new French vans with their refined diesel engines and they became favourite choices for buyers.

The Talbot Express launched after the discontinuation of the Dodge Spacevan, which had essentially existed as the Commer van from 1962. The Express became a firm favourite for campervan conversions, with many of the UK converters using it until the Talbot badge was dropped in 1993. As the 1980s moved into the 1990s new versions of Ford's Transit and the VW Transporter became top choices for converters. During this period there was still a market of DIY converters, with some manufacturers of campervans continuing to

The Renault Traffic was used by Holdsworth on the new Romance. Holdsworth had gained an excellent reputation for quality campervans.

VW had launched a 4 x 4 version of its Transporter in the mid-1980s and Renault followed with this 4 x 4 Traffic in 1986. It was very capable by the looks of it!

supply furniture kits and GRP moulded high-top roofs. Another popular option was to buy a pre-owned van for converting into a new campervan.

Some names that are around today, such as Murvi and Bilbo's, began as small concerns in the 1980s, converting VWs and building their markets over the years. Auto-Sleepers was using Talbots and VW for its campervans of the period and Citroën the C25. Dormobile, which had in many ways been a pioneer of the campervan, had been owned by the Coalite Group and Charrington. By the early 1980s it was beset with financial problems and in 1994 this once-great name was forced to close the previously thriving plant in Kiln Lane, which was then sadly demolished.

The 1990s saw the arrival of new converters and more updated van bases, VW remaining a firm favourite. In 1993 IH, now a well-established converter, began along with Nu Venture. This decade saw the campervan gaining popularity again and also heralded change. Autohomes UK became a force again within the industry, with new models launched such as the high-top Karisma, its specification including a TV. A VW-based conversion, Autohomes also used Ford and even Nissan under Elddis. Key figure Iain Macpherson's untimely death saw Autohomes UK run into problems having been bought by Elddis Caravans in 1990. After a few years the company dropped campervans and the name and closed the Poole factory.

Auto-Sleepers had experimented with several bases and used the Talbot Express for the 1989 high-top Rambler model, seen here.

Above: The VW-based Karisma was one of several new designs brought out by Autohomes UK following its formation in 1983.

Left: Freight Rover joined forces with Auto-Sleeper in 1983 to develop the Sherpa Leisure campervan. VW, Ford and Commer knew that sales of campervans aided general commercial van sales.

Imported coach-built vehicles had begun to appear and also several campervans from Hobby as well as a few US imports. Auto-Sleepers and Holdsworth entered the 1990s in strong positions. In 1983 Auto-Sleepers joined forces with Freight Rover to produce a 2-litre petrol engine with elevating roof named Sherpa Leisure; it came well equipped at £8,126. Auto-Sleepers had used the Sherpa from its launch in 1975. The 1990s would see improved van bases with VW and Ford's ever-popular Transit all updated. The Fiat Ducato was gaining ground with converters and this included Murvi using it with their Meteor, a rear-end-lounge layout with side kitchen. The Meteor was a popular model with Murvi and by the early 1990s the company had a strong foothold in the campervan market.

Layouts with campervans had developed in line with the changes in the van models available and with new smaller accessories, compact kitchens could be practical too. With twin-burner hobs and combined oven/grills, small fridges and better 12-V lighting, campervans were more appealing than ever, selling on the lifestyle of 'go virtually anywhere' touring. Coach-builts were more bulky in size and not as easy to drive, so campervans were ideal for many. Sales would increase in the mid-1980s as the economy began to grow again.

The number of dealerships that had stopped trading by the mid-1990s was high in number. This included some of the larger concerns or those that swapped over to car sales. Back then few caravan dealers sold both caravans and campervans, unlike nowadays when

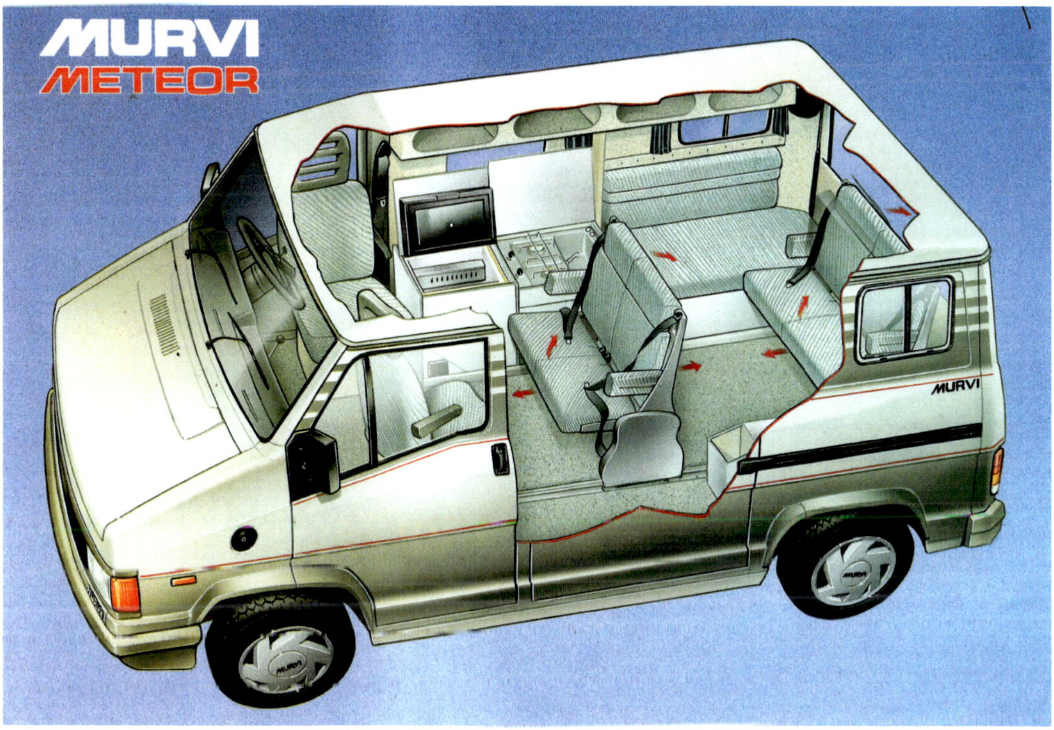

Based in Devon, Murvi was originally known as Nomadic Wheels, changing its name to Murvi in the 1990s.

this is commonplace. Turner's of London had become well established and would also carry out conversions on request. Today Turner's is an MOT centre – it's difficult to imagine it was once a formidable force in campervan retail. Small dealer concerns still sprang up and grew over the years, Spinney Group being a prime example. However, many smaller converters would sell direct to the customer, thus cutting out the dealer. Companies such as Leisuredrive (established in 1969) covered the high-top and elevating roof market and also offered a lower high-top-model range, with the glass-fibre moulded roof tops being manufactured at their factory, which continues today.

A 1990s advert for Turner's, a prolific campervan dealership in their day.

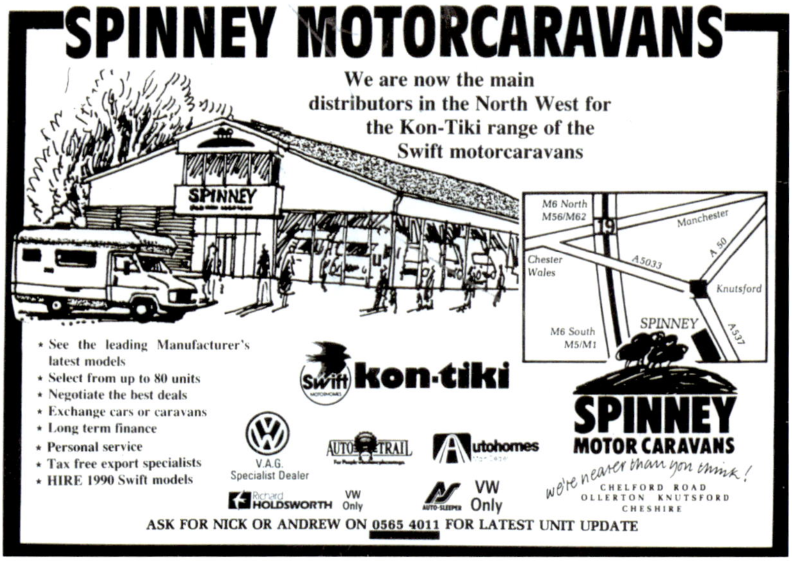

Established in 1975, Spinney is a business run by the Holland family and over the fifty years of its existence has expanded to six dealerships. This advert dates from the early 1990s when there was just one branch in Cheshire.

Right: By 1994 Leisuredrive had become popular with campervan buyers, who appreciate the company's sound, practical designs. The company produce kits for DIY converters and have their own glass-fibre mould shop.

Below: Nu Venture Motorhomes began in 1993 and soon began scooping up awards for its campervans. This is the 2006 Dia using a Fiat Scuda van.

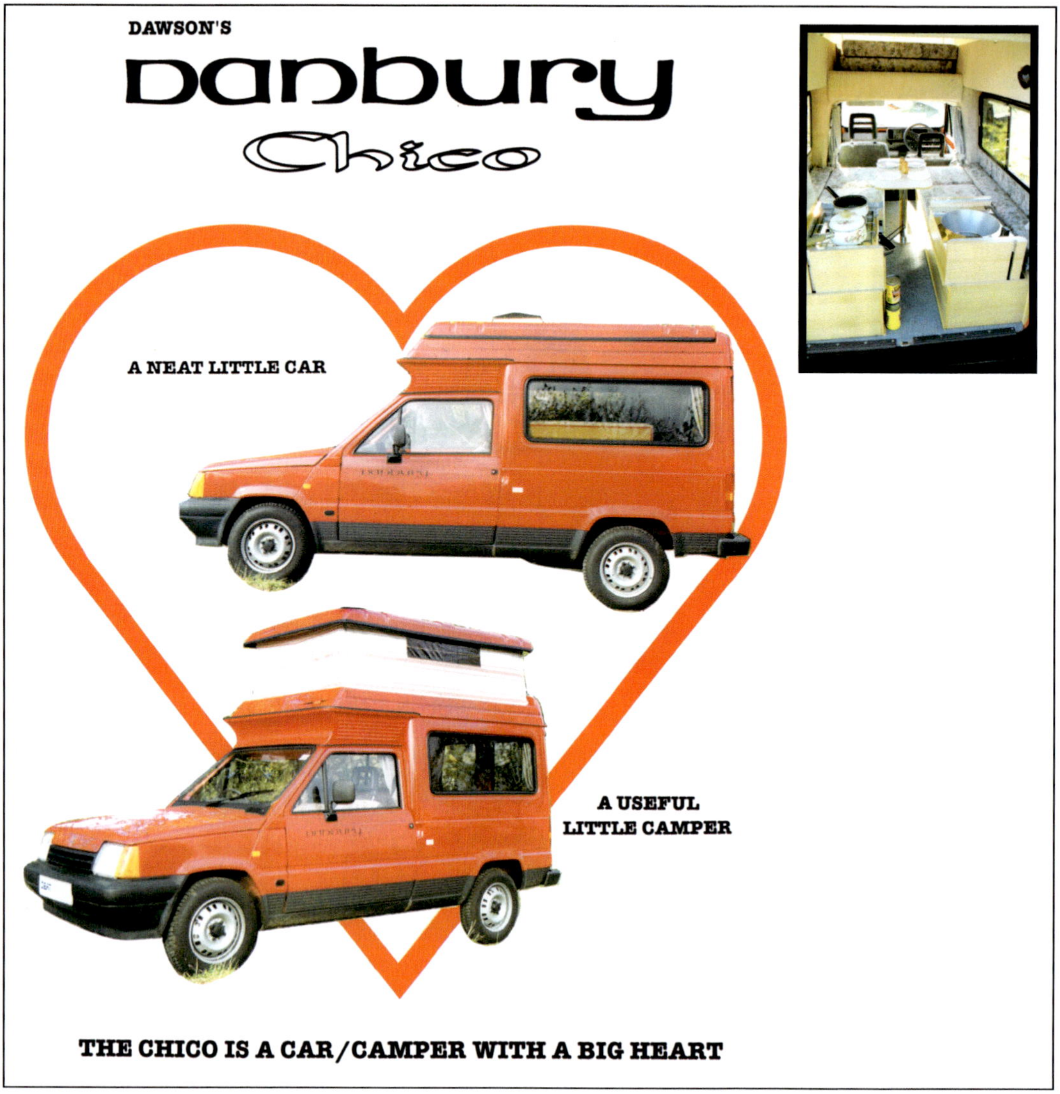

In 1991 Danbury used the Seat Terra, a 1.3 diesel-powered van, for the cheeky Chico, which slept two.

Nu Venture began in 1993, making small coach-builts as well as doing conversions. The company has built a strong reputation based on quality, personal service and award-winning layouts using Fiat, Peugeot and Citroën. West Country Conversions, based in Exmouth, began in 1985 and although not prolific, its well-specified campervans have found a niche in a large campervan market where each maker has its own unique selling point.

Campervans were appealing to those who wanted easy travel accompanied by home comforts and a regular form of transport during the working week. The Danbury (renamed Dawson's Danbury) company produced its chic micro-camper based on a Seat Terra using a 1.3 diesel, featuring an elevating roof and sleeping two in 1991. Micro-campervans, although

Above left: The West Country Kestrel VW conversion. This small maker has been producing quality, well-specified campervans since 1985.

Above right: The popular Auto-Sleepers Trooper high-top conversion from 1997.

a niche market, did have a following particularly among couples. Tandy Industries added an Austin Maestro van as a conversion.

Auto-Sleepers, which came under the Marquis dealership and then later French leisure group Trigano, produced some of the best sellers in the 1990s with models such as Trooper and Trident, which by the mid-1990s were based on the latest VW Transporters. Autocruise, based in South Yorkshire, would eventually move from coach-builts to van conversions too, with Swift buying the company and making high-top campervans. In 1993 Swift

Above left: Swift launched its first campervan, a VW-based high-top called the Carrera, in 1993.

Above right: The Fiat Ducato-based Mondial high-top was another campervan venture by Swift.

introduced its Carrera high-top on a VW, a name that would reappear some years later in the Swift campervan portfolio. By 1995/6 Swift used the Fiat Ducato to launch a new campervan, the Mondial, a high-top. It wasn't until a few years later when they purchased Autocruise motorhomes that they returned to campervan conversions.

More caravan sites were catering for the campervan and motorhome and provided level pitches. Both clubs now accepted the campervan readily and the major shows had

Above: Campervan life was a different ball game in the early days when vans were smaller and far more basic than this Vanmaster Troodos from 2005.

Left: The slide-out extending idea hasn't been a big hit in the UK. This is a 2003 Manhattan using a Fiat Ducato van; the company only lasted a few years.

Wellhouse Leisure began in 2003 and went on to convert Toyota, Mazda, Hyundai and Ford. This is the Hi-Ace-based Granvia elevating-roof conversion.

more new models and converters in attendance. The 2000s saw the campervan enter a new era. With improved vehicle bases and diesel being the preferred engine, more powerful and refined units attracted greater numbers to the campervan way of life. The days of underpowered and cramped conversions were for many a distant memory. New ideas and designs in the last part of this story demonstrate that the campervan has won more fans. Extending sides in campervans helped to create more space. The Manhattan, based on a Fiat 2.8 JTD, had a slide-out and a luxury finish. Other makers also tried this idea, but it had few takers and proved not to be a success in the UK.

New concerns would crop up in the 2000s and some are still in business today. Wellhouse Leisure was established in 2003 and began by converting Mazda Bongos and Toyota Hi-Ace and Hyundai vans. The company has grown and become well known in the campervan market. Hillside, formed in 2007/8, have taken the campervan market by storm over the years, using the latest VW Transporter. The campervan market has also witnessed more self-builds over the last twenty years, a practice that seems more popular than ever with some firms starting out in this fashion. VW marketed the Californian converted by Westfalia (but VW would do their own conversion) and using that name, but in 2012 VW dropped Westfalia and the California emerged also on a VW Caddy and the VW Crafter, adding more choice.

The 2000s have also seen a dramatic increase in imported makes of campers from names such as Adria, Hymer, Hobby, Westfalia, Globecar, Reimor, Dethleffs, Knaus, Trigano, Benimar and La Strada, providing an extensive choice of models for the UK buyer.

The VW Californian, once converted by Westfalia and now by VW, has a cult following among modern campervan buyers.

The ever-growing number of small converters across the UK, including several in Scotland, shows just how popular campervan life is. Many owners now write about their experience and live in their campers as a way of life. This would have been unheard of in the early part of the campervan story, when a round trip to Land's End and John o'Groats in a VW T2 Devon campervan was seen as a marathon!

It is also interesting how caravan manufacturers over the period of this story converted some of those early campervans and that in modern times Bailey, Elddis and Swift along with Coachman are now firmly in the campervan market. In 2013/14 Lunar Caravans was one of the first to convert campervans, using the Mercedes long wheelbase for their Landstar RL, a luxury campervan. The company also entered the compact campervan market, using a Nissan NV200 incorporating an elevating roof design and a blow-up mattress for the bed. Named the Vacanza, it didn't sell very well, possibly because of it being on a Nissan instead of one of the French van bases.

Nowadays the campervan is a very modern leisure vehicle with solar panels, LED lighting, flush toilets, mains electrics and main converters building to legislation and higher tolerances. The Covid-19 pandemic in 2020 would set the leisure-vehicle industry on a real sales surge with demand outstripping supply. More families would take up the campervan life, meaning children could enjoy freedom with few restrictions. New converters set up many small concerns while many purchased a good used delivery van (though prices on those rocketed too) and began fitting them out. There were many good examples and few not so.

Above: Bailey entered the campervan market with its Endeavour high-top using the latest Ford Transit as its base.

Below: Swift Trekkers on the line in the dedicated factory for campervan production at Swifts' Cottingham complex.

Above: The interior of Elddis' CV20. The company's campervans have become popular since their launch in 2019 and for a while they also made a Compass model version.

Below: Lunar Caravans entered the campervan market with a Mercedes-based model, the Landstar. It had limited success and their 2013 Nissan-based Vacanza micro-camper, seen here, also received a lukewarm reception.

During the Covid-19 pandemic many families were attracted to the campervan life as a way of getting away and staying safe from the virus.

The market was booming and prices also began to rise with customers often outbidding another to buy a van. The problem was also made worse as the new converter concerns wanted the same prices as established makers. This saw the advent of over-inflated prices, which buyers were eager to pay to enable them to get away from it all and enjoy a holiday of sorts. As soon as the government restrictions began to be lifted two years down the line, the market began to slow but was geared up to higher production. By 2024 the market had returned to pre-Covid levels but had to deal with the issue of too many campervans being available.

Some of the one-man bands have packed up and others will no doubt follow given the high cost of living, expensive vehicle bases and energy prices. This will inevitably lead to a slow down in the market. However, the market has seen that early retirees are increasingly considering the campervan option, especially with the way that modern day vans drive like cars in many cases. Sites such as YouTube feature vlogs by campervan owners eager to tell of their adventures and encourage others to join them. The campervan lifestyle began over seventy years ago with the VW Kombi and Westfalia, a caravan maker in Germany, coming up with the idea of an all-purpose vehicle that would enable many to enjoy an inexpensive holiday

With modern manufacturing the latest campervans are a world apart from those early Dormobiles and the other pioneering makes. However, without some of those names the

Above: Many of the latest generation of campervan owners vlog about where they go and recommend places to stop over. In some places it is possible to park overnight, which some users find appealing.

Below: Auto-Sleepers' Ford Transit-based Air campervan. Now under the French Trigano Group as UK maker Autotrail, the Auto-Sleepers' identity is kept separate.

campervan may not have progressed as it did to what it has become today. With dealer specials and customised models, the choice today is endless. The VW Kombi was the founder of the campervan and in the UK it was down to enterprising folk to take a risk to make the campervan idea a commercial success. Shows that displayed those early converters are still an important part of the campervan story as they allow buyers to see a good range of new models highlighting the latest in campervan design.

Right: An early VW conversion by European Cars, London, *c.* 1959. Companies like this helped develop the campervan idea.

Below: In the modern campervan era shows have an important role to play in allowing would-be buyers to see the latest in campervan design.

The campervan story will no doubt carry on evolving further but owes a great deal to the early days when Peter Pitt's ingenuity with layout and Dormobile's promotion of the campervan helped to bring it to the public's attention. The campervan can become for many a way to escape from the stresses of everyday modern life and to extend their hobbies. Predicting the future of this leisure vehicle, all-electric campervans may be the way forward. Scottish converter Campervan Co. have the Eco Revolution model all ready for the future, mindful of the 2030 proposed ban on the selling of new combustion engines in the UK. One thing for sure is that the campervan story is a fascinating and forever evolving one and with electric vehicles and several converters already providing both all-electric and hybrid models, the campervan looks set for another exciting chapter in its history.

The all-electric Eco Revolution by Campervan Co., a Scottish company. No gas is required here – is this the future of the campervan?